The
Street
Where
I
Live

H V Kershaw

The
Street
Where
I
Live

GRANADA
London Toronto Sydney New York

Granada Publishing Limited
Frogmore, St Albans, Herts AL2 2NF
and
36 Golden Square, London W1R 4AH
866 United Nations Plaza, New York, NY 10017, USA
117 York Street, Sydney, NSW 2000, Australia
100 Skyway Avenue, Rexdale, Ontario M9W 3A6, Canada
61 Beach Road, Auckland, New Zealand

Published by Granada Publishing 1981

Copyright © H. V. Kershaw 1981

ISBN 0 246 11734 6

Printed in Great Britain by
Richard Clay (The Chaucer Press) Ltd,
Bungay, Suffolk

Granada ®
Granada Publishing ®

Foreword

Any chronicle of *Coronation Street* must inevitably be a history of popular television. The programme, only four years younger than ITV itself, has triumphantly survived major changes in technology, artistic fashion and social behaviour. It has employed hundreds of artists, dozens of writers, vast numbers of producers, directors, production assistants, floor managers, stage managers, cameramen, designers, carpenters, stage hands, make-up artists, wardrobe mistresses, casting directors, property men, lighting supervisors, sound engineers and secretaries. It has been both the joy and the bane of a changing band of Granada executives. And throughout its long life it has enjoyed the unfailing loyalty of over half the viewing population of the British Isles.

It has been my pleasure to serve *Coronation Street* as scriptwriter, editor, novelist, producer and executive producer. I can only hope that this account of that service will be as entertaining in the reading as it was in the living.

H. V. KERSHAW
1981

Acknowledgements

The author and publisher thank the following for permission to quote from copyright material:
Brian Cowgill; *Encyclopaedia Britannica*; and Granada Television for the script extracts in Chapter 12.

CHAPTER ONE

'Don't talk to me about the old days! They're best forgotten!'

Ena Sharples

At 2 pm on Tuesday, 12 January 1971 I rose to my feet in the Lancaster Room of London's Savoy Hotel to respond to a toast. The occasion, a celebration by the Variety Club of the tenth birthday of a television phenomenon; the toast *'Coronation Street'*; my role the programme's executive producer. As I gazed at the sea of famous faces around me only one thought echoed and re-echoed in my mind – how on *earth* did I get here?

It all began, as do so many things, with Mother. When I was a young child mine was forever taking me to the pictures, not because she loved me – although she did – but because she was the most passionate devotee of the silver screen that I have ever known. Beside my mother, Barry Norman and Philip Jenkinson are casual dabblers in the cinematic arts. In the corner shop, asked who was the chap who played opposite what's-her-name in that funny picture about gangsters, my mother would answer, without hesitation, 'Chester Morris!' And she'd be right.

My frequent trips to the cinema always began in the same way. The house would be quiet, the tea things cleared away from the table where I would be sitting with my Scout Annual, mopping up some camping hints that I would never put into practice whilst my father, puffing his pipe, would be immersed in a crossword puzzle and my sister polished her nails for the evening's encounter with the boyfriend. We knew the signs. My mother would fidget for a moment then lay down her knitting, stand, look at me resignedly and say, 'Go on then, get your school cap and I'll take you to the Savoy.' The word 'then' was not only carefully chosen but totally unfair. It implied that ever since I came home from school I had been pestering to be taken to the pictures whereas nothing could have been farther from the truth. However, I played the game, not only because I loved my mother but because even at that tender age I was turning into a fair old cinema buff myself.

There were times when my mother miscalculated. Most of the films she took me to see at the Savoy Cinematograph Hall were fit material for a young impressionable mind but there were occasions when the villain was a little too villainous and his deeds a little too horrific and it was then that my head would drop and I would stare into the blackness between my feet. My eyes would close, waiting for the moment to pass but before it could I would sense my mother leaning towards me, feel her head near my shoulder and hear her whispered comforting words, 'It's only a story.'

Realities in Britain during the late 1920s and early 1930s were a far cry from the world of John Gilbert and Vilma Banky, Edward Everett Horton and Ramon Novarro. The country was deep into its worst depression and the vultures were moving in. In those days my father worked as a Senior Pattern Card Maker in a cotton warehouse in central Manchester and already he was conniving at his own downfall. I can hear him now as he rubbed his hands in front of the kitchen fire: 'Moved myself a bit nearer the dole queue again today.' We knew what to expect. 'Showed another party of Japs around the place. By gum, they're a clever lot! They're taking it all in.' A sigh, then: 'We must be mad.' He. knew what was coming but like so many of his kind he felt powerless to stop it. In a matter of years his words had come true. The Japanese had gone home and built their mills and their warehouses and had trained men to do my father's job. For a fraction of his meagre pay.

It was into this atmosphere that I stepped, my school days behind me, to earn a living. I had enjoyed every moment of my years as a scholarship boy at Hulme Grammar School (now William Hulme's) but to pursue my academic career was unthinkable. Money needed to be earned and I set about looking for a job. A good mark in mathematics led me surprisingly quickly to a 'position of responsibility and high future prospects' with a motor insurance company. As a junior clerk. At 12s 6d per week.

But the firm went bankrupt and I jumped at the opportunity to join the Prudential where I stayed until the war claimed me. My mother had died two years previously and I was living with my father when the call to arms plopped through our letter-box. I was to report to the 341st Machine Gun Training Centre at Alderney, the remotest of the Channel Islands and as far away as I could get from home and still remain in the British Isles. On 14 January 1940 I said my farewells and went to war.

My travels as a soldier took me far and wide: to South Africa and India, Iraq, Iran, Israel, Syria and Egypt; to Sicily, Italy, France, Belgium and Germany where, in May 1945, my war ended not two miles from the spot where Monty lent the shattered German generals his fountain pen, and peace returned to Europe.

During the war the Prudential had made up the pay of all those members of its staff who had awaited the call-up before joining the forces. I don't know what it cost them but no doubt they saw it as a gamble on the integrity of their employees and when, in late 1945 and the spring of 1946 the soldiers, the sailors and the airmen began drifting back to civilian life, they reaped their winnings. Most of these staff returned to their desks and exchanged the trappings of a six-year war, not for the brave new world for which they had fought but for the same old timid one that they had left behind. I ran with the herd.

If the business side of my life was a trifle dull during those immediate post-war years, the same cannot be said for the social side. In October 1946 I met the woman who was to become my wife in October the following year. In December 1948 our daughter arrived.

I had met my wife at the Players' Dramatic Society, an amateur company in Cheadle Hulme, the Cheshire village/suburb where I had gone to live with my sister and her husband after I was demobilized. Here I began to act and, after a presentation of *The Winslow Boy* for which we were severely mangled by the local press, to write. My first play was a light-hearted, but none the less vindictive stab at drama critics. Naturally enough it was performed with high glee by the Society itself and I was encouraged to expand my playwriting career. Although never as prolific as Ernie Wise I began churning out plays, long and short, at a quite alarming rate. The Society, much to their credit and as evidence of their undoubted bravery, performed most of them and the time came when my plays were even winning prizes at local festivals. Further encouraged, I submitted a selection to a firm of publishers and to my immense joy three were accepted. This, I felt, was truly the culmination of all my efforts.

I never thought for a single moment of approaching the BBC. Somehow I never felt that they dealt with my kind of stuff and, in any event, I was quite happy fulfilling my dramatic career by acting for the Players on the one hand and collecting the meagre but magical royalties on my published plays on the other. And then, in 1955, along came Independent Television.

Two companies – Granada and ABC – set up their creative headquarters in Manchester. I decided to concentrate my attack on Granada and sent them my three published plays together with a little note saying that this was a sample of what I could do and asking if they would like to meet me. Within a few days a formal note arrived fixing an interview at their Water Street offices.

The interview was a huge disappointment. I was interrogated by a young man who obviously knew quite as much about television as I did and who, though polite, held out no hope. However, if I were ever to write anything else . . . He let the words dangle and when I got back home and started to think about it I was pretty sure that if he'd finished the sentence he'd have told me to keep it to myself. On to ABC!

ABC were totally different. I sent the same three published plays to them and waited and waited and waited for a reply. Not for them the prompt formality of Granada and I had begun to give up hope when the jackpot burst open at my feet. A letter arrived telling me that they were greatly interested in two of my three plays and would I like to go along and talk business with them.

At that time ABC had the weekend franchise, and all their Manchester affairs were carried out on either the Saturday or the Sunday of each week. I had a Saturday morning appointment and I can recall my wife giving me a last brush down and an encouraging kiss before I boarded the bus to take me to Didsbury.

A polite Commissionaire greeted me in what once had been the cinema's foyer and rang through for George Kerr, the script editor of ABC's *Armchair Theatre* and the man I was to meet. A couple of moments later George, a smiling Australian, emerged from the bowels of the building, walked towards me and shook me warmly by the hand. 'Come into the office,' he said. My feet involuntarily took me three or four paces into the building before I realized that Mr Kerr had gone the other way. I turned and saw the outer door swinging and George's back disappearing down the steps. Throwing a confused smile at the Commissionaire I decided to join in this strange game and, dashing out and rushing across the road, just caught George as he was about to enter the saloon bar of the Parrswood Hotel. There he ordered two pints of bitter, found us seats at what was presumably his office table near the window and proceeded to talk turkey. This, I decided, was more like it.

My stay with ABC was short but very sweet. A deal had been quickly struck over *Flashpoint*, one of the three plays I had submitted, the fee offered was acceptable – let's face it, *any* fee would have been acceptable – and in no time at all my wife and I went along on a dreamlike Sunday night to see the play transmitted. Of course, this was long before videotape and if the play was billed in the *TV Times* as starting at nine o'clock that was the time it started in the studio. I had been to earlier rehearsals, and had met Stuart Latham, the director, who was to become a good friend and colleague. Harry, as he was better known, was no stranger to Manchester. He had been a guiding light at the beginning of Manchester's Library Theatre and was greatly respected amongst the theatrical community. And feared by a few of them. A man of acid wit, he had never been able to suffer fools gladly, but an innate diplomacy and a calm efficiency enabled him to sit relaxedly in the control room and, his eyes screwed against the drifting smoke from his ever-present cigarette, preside over the madhouse of a television production as if he were taking tea in some British residency East of Suez.

Whilst *Flashpoint* was in rehearsal, George Kerr opened negotiations on a second play, *The Hollow Crown*. Again, and not surprisingly, we reached agreement and in a few weeks' time I achieved a minor distinction by becoming the first writer to have a second play on *Armchair Theatre*.

High with such heady success I was beginning to wonder if perhaps life held more for me than paying claims to weeping widows and whether in fact my future lay with ABC Television when, suddenly, all my contacts disappeared into thin air. Harry Latham joined Granada, George Kerr went back home to lie on Bondi Beach, and my second director was, I found, a freelance who had now left the company and was back working for the BBC. This was a crushing blow and for several months I licked my wounds.

It needed luck and the interest of James Ormerod, a Granada programme director, to set me once more on the yellow brick road. Jimmy Ormerod read my published plays, declared his interest and arranged my first meeting with Harry Elton, Granada's Executive Producer of Drama. Harry, an expansive Canadian, in every sense of the adjective, had been one of the first flight of wild colonial boys to descend on England at the inception of ITV. How much know-how and experience they brought with them was questionable, but they undoubtedly furnished an enthusiasm and a zest for work which was invaluable in those early days.

This was a different Granada from the one I had known. Suddenly it was a television station and no longer the cold stockbrokers' office I had thought it to be. Harry Elton's gusto made an immediate impression and I left his office after our first meeting with a firm commission to write an episode of *Shadow Squad*. This was the way not only to capture but to stimulate anyone's imagination.

The heady days returned. For some inexplicable reason the Prudential had transferred me and for an entire winter I commuted into Manchester by one train and out the other side by another to Bolton. A couple of nights each week on the way home I would stop off in Manchester, have my meetings with either Harry Elton or Denis Forman (now Sir Denis, then Granada's Programme Controller), about my commission of the moment, go back home and, after a quick meal, sit down at my typewriter until three o'clock the following morning. Up again at six and the whole process would start again.

Not unnaturally this became rather wearing and my wife and I started serious talks about the possibility of my giving up one career or the other. There was no doubt in my mind which of the two, writing or insurance, I wished to pursue but I had a wife and daughter to support and the thought of giving up a secure pensionable job for the imponderables of television scriptwriting was not one I could easily accept. The question of some kind of contract with Granada had been raised with both Harry Elton and Denis Forman over the preceding months but neither would commit himself in any way. I was told that there just weren't any writers under contract to independent companies.

The choice could have been agonizing had it not been for my wife, who cast her vote firmly for adventure. In May 1960 I resigned from the Prudential, my wife gave up her teaching job, we moved house and bought a new car. My father, taught to worship at the shrine of security, must have turned in his grave.

My resignation had been submitted on a Friday and that evening I wasn't fit to live with. The die had been cast, the last bridge burnt and I was in the grip of a gang of unscrupulous entrepreneurs who would bleed me dry and chuck me out within the year. My wife suggested I should go and see Harry Elton and tell him what I had done. I rang Harry and within half an hour I was sitting in his den with a drink in my hand.

'I just thought I would tell you that in a month's time if you want to talk about a script you'll be able to do it in more civilized hours,' I said. 'I have given up my nine to five job and I'll be – guess what – a full time writer.'

He lifted his glass. 'Great,' he said. 'Now we must start thinking about a contract.'

Before my notice had expired, I was the proud owner of a contract with Granada Television to write for such programmes as they wished up to a guaranteed sum far in excess of my insurance earnings.

In the event, things were vastly better. During the first contractual year I earned twice as much as I had been guaranteed. As far as my previous employers were concerned, they accepted my resignation without a word, returned twenty-five years worth of personal pension contributions without a penny of interest, and that was that. Many people asked at the time how I could be so stupid as to exchange the family atmosphere of insurance for the rat-race of television. I pointed out gently that the opposite was the case.

It soon became evident that a writing contract which guaranteed work up to a certain financial level was a very beneficial document indeed. I was never short of work. During those early years I wrote for *Shadow Squad*, *Skyport*, *The Verdict Is Yours* and *In Court Today* and by the late summer of 1960 I had added a couple of play adaptations and several highly enjoyable episodes of *Biggles*, the children's adventure series, and was then writing for *Knight Errant*, a light-hearted and somewhat upper-middle-class crime series. Granada had given me a small office in the building, and I was sharpening a scene or two in my current script when the telephone rang. It was Harry Latham, director of my first play on television and more recently my producer on *Biggles*.

'I don't know whether you know,' he said, 'but they've asked me to produce this new North of England serial. They want me to do twenty-six episodes. Would you like to script edit for me?'

I had arrived. I had followed the yellow brick road from the Savoy Cinematograph Hall and there I was, although I didn't know it then, on the threshold of the longest street in the world.

CHAPTER TWO

'There's a lot to think of, running a shop.'

Florrie Lindley

Great events, we are led to believe, cast their shadows before them, but to say that the phenomenal success of *Coronation Street* was in any way evident from the outset, would be to tell a lie.

The approach to the new venture was low key although there were many, including myself, who would, if pressed to a psychiatrist's couch, admit to some slight stirring of the blood at our first encounter with the serial.

There had certainly never been anything like it before. Not that this was any guarantee of its success. Television was, and still is, littered with unique failures. What, then, separated *Coronation Street* from the rest? What was it that stirred our blood? To begin with it was 'different' in a different way. Whereas most writers claimed novelty for their creations by pushing them further and further into the realms of fantasy, here was a brain child which moved nearer, much nearer, to real life and real people. The programme had been sold on the strength of five half-hour scripts and they were a delight to read. The characterization was superb and at the end of the first five episodes, you *knew* Elsie Tanner and Ena Sharples and Ken Barlow and his family and little Lucille Hewitt and her widower father. You closed your eyes and you could see the pot flight of ducks and the antimacassars and the chenille table cloths and the newspapers stuffed under the cushion of the easy chair. You sniffed and you could smell the burning sausages and the cheap hair spray and the tang of bitter beer.

Those first scripts laid a solid foundation for everything that was to follow. There is not the slightest doubt about it, the credit for the success of *Coronation Street* must first go to Tony Warren, the young, fair-haired ex-actor with the superb ear for dialogue and an undoubted devotion for the streets and the people of his native Salford. Granada was fortunate indeed that he was working in their Promotion Department at the time he wrote these first scripts. But the company had its part to play, too. If Tony Warren had worked a miracle in holding up the mirror to the millions who had lived or were still living in the Coronation Streets of Britain, the next marvel was that Granada accepted the idea.

This creation, this 'volume of unwritten rules', as Tony Warren called it in his foreword, had, on the face of it, very little going for it. These were the days of escapism, the evenings spent with *Maigret* and *Tim Frazer*, *Gary Halliday* and the boys from *Bonanza*. Where in this world of fantasy lay the space for the trivia of *Coronation Street*? But space was found – and found, I suggest, because of one essential difference between then and now. In those days Granada was ruled by creative men to whom contracts and money were sordid companions in the adventure. It was a well-known fact that any writer worth his salt could write a ninety-minute play before the company could draft a one-page contract, but somehow it didn't matter. What was important then was making programmes. In television today, as in so many areas of British business life, the accountants rule the roost. I venture to guess that had Tony Warren submitted *Coronation Street* to the Independent Television of 1981 the programme would never have been made. Happily – and not least for Granada – he beat the system by twenty years.

In spite of the buccaneering spirit which prevailed in those days, the adoption of Tony's idea still came as something of a shock to some people in Granada. The tiny production team, Harry Latham as producer, myself as script editor, and Tony himself as writer, was careful, however, not to be carried away on a cloud of euphoria. We all knew that the war was far from won. There were still elements – and powerful elements – in Granada who honestly believed that no programme could be a success without a strong and obvious middle-class appeal. We were to learn later that the programme did indeed have a middle-class appeal but it wasn't obvious at the time, and there were those who tried hard to inject 'classier' ingredients into the programme. Our David to these Goliaths was Harry Latham, a redoubtable fighter at all levels. Whilst, during the few months run-up to transmission, Tony and I worked on the next seven scripts which Tony was to write, Harry spent his time warding off attacks from those who believed that no self-respecting solicitor and his family would derive the slightest entertainment from the goings on in a working-class street. Let one thing be made absolutely clear. We were not fighting enemies of the programme. Had this been the case the battle would have been so much the easier but this was the worst kind of civil war with everyone loving the somewhat squalid territory over which they were fighting. Everyone concerned simply wished to make the programme as good as we could possibly make it. The only problem was that we had different ways of going about it. But Tony Warren and I, raised in the working-class streets of Salford and Manchester, knew that our way was right and we supplied the ammunition for our London-born producer to fire. And he fired them so successfully that the second name on the *Coronation Street* roll of honour must assuredly be that of Harry Latham, without whose arguments and winning ways the programme would have lost a great deal of its truth and without doubt most of its life.

I remember him coming into my office one afternoon after a particularly rough session. 'They're wearing me down,' he said. 'They want a young doctor living at No. 5. They say he'll add bloom, whatever that is.' For a moment or two we lived in a defeated silence, before I dredged a word from my memory.

'You savages from the South may not know this,' I told him, 'but up here in the North bloom is an unsightly deposit caused by outside influences.'

I was about to add 'usually on furniture', when he stopped me. 'Don't tell me any more,' he said, 'that's quite enough!' and he went upstairs, told his critics that bloom was an unsightly deposit caused by outside influences and we never heard of the young doctor again.

During this run-up period, activity was intense. The production team had been strengthened by a trio of programme directors, Mike Scott, Derek Bennett and Eric Price and a designer, Denis Parkin. This quartet, possibly the busiest four people in Granada at that time, were engaged in a multiplicity of activities – casting, camera tests, design problems, scheduling, the choice of the technical team and the preparation of camera scripts among them. But this was a team effort and we all found ourselves involved. One day I would be bowling along the streets of Salford with Denis Parkin looking for the ideal architecture for our street, the next sitting in a rehearsal room at Granada with a panel of judges auditioning streams of would-be Harry Hewitts and Minnie Caldwells. At the time these were merely jobs and we had no idea how far-reaching our decisions were to be. As an example, we chose Archie Street in Salford as a template for our own street. By this I mean that we simply adopted certain characteristics of the houses; the small, downstairs bay window, the single front door step, that sort of thing. There was never any question that any of the lives, loves, births and deaths of *Coronation Street* were connected in any way with the inhabitants of Archie Street, but the Press and other interested parties had different ideas. Frank Allaun MP, the parliamentary representative for Archie Street, announced himself as *Coronation Street*'s MP and when, a few years ago, Archie Street was demolished to make way for high-rise flats, the Press screamed: 'Is this the end of *Coronation Street*?' Of course it wasn't because *Coronation Street* was no one street. We all had our ideas but the only common factor was that it lay within a fifteen-mile radius of Granada's studios in Manchester. Tony Warren, when pressed for more accuracy, would merely wave his arm vaguely towards the studio window and say: 'It's out there somewhere.' And that's just where it was.

The most frenzied activity of those pre-production days was, without doubt, casting the twenty-four running parts which had appeared in the first five episodes. Some were big, some were small, but all were equally important in the eyes of those responsible for ensuring that the part went to the right artist. Margaret Morris, the casting director, and Josie Scott, her assistant, combed the repertory companies of the North and Midlands looking for suitable material. There was a good reason for this. Normally parts are cast by memory or from the pages of *Spotlight*, the actors' directory, but it had been decided at producer level that we should as far as possible avoid known faces. If you are to ask your audience to see Elsie Tanner, Ena Sharples and Annie Walker as real people, you couldn't in all conscience cast them from the ranks of faces which had appeared and re-appeared on television over the years. This was a pity in many ways as British television was blessed with a very large corps of excellent actors and actresses, but *Coronation Street* was to discover that there were many others who were deserving of the chance to join their ranks.

Casting sessions were an agonizing ordeal, not only for the artist being auditioned, who must have been scared to death at seeing such a frightening array of people (there were never fewer than seven on the auditioning panel), but for the panel themselves who tried to sleep at night by counting endless streams of Florrie Lindleys jumping over shop counters. It could have been much much worse. We could have been undecided and argued endlessly about the casting of every character but, surprisingly, practically all Tony Warren's creations cast themselves when it came to the point. When Pat Phoenix arrived to read Elsie Tanner there was really no point in asking anyone else to bother; when Arthur Leslie read the part of Jack Walker the part was his almost from the first sentence; and when Doris Speed bestowed her gracious smile on the hard-eyed panel and began to create a flesh and blood Annie Walker, we knew that the end of that particular trail was in sight. The only character who gave us any trouble was that of Ena Sharples. All of us, producer, script editor, directors and casting directors alike had envisaged her as small and scrawny, thin-lipped and vinegary and this description had produced a limited number of applicants, none of whom seemed quite right. It was only after Tony Warren had recommended that we should see Violet Carson that we realized our identikit picture of Ena Sharples had been totally wrong. We must have been mad – how could we possibly have thought of anyone else?

Whilst casting has always been one of the most important facets of television production, the casting of a serial like *Coronation Street* was crucial. Not only would the right artist play the part well but he or she would determine the growth of the character. One shining example of the truth of this theory presented itself at this time. I have said that 'practically' all Tony Warren's creations cast themselves but there were one or two where the panel was left undecided between two or three applicants. The part of Dennis Tanner was a case in point. Both Philip Lowrie and Ken Farrington, two clever young actors of the day, had their champions and it was decided that both should be camera-tested for the part. Philip Lowrie was eventually chosen after a great deal of argument and counter-argument and there, apparently, the matter rested. A simple choice had been made between. two very efficient actors. But what would have happened had the position been reversed and Ken Farrington had landed the role of Dennis Tanner, as well he might? The strong possibility is that the character would have developed along the lines of its original creation – that of a vicious tearaway who had only recently left approved school. What in fact happened was that after two or three episodes of Dennis Tanner as played by Philip Lowrie we changed course, excused his previous lapses on the grounds that he was weak and easily led, and turned him into a zany, head-in-the-sky kid, thirsting after a career in show-business. This suited us as, juvenile delinquency being one of the biggest clichés on the British television screen at that time, we all preferred to ignore it for the time being. And that wasn't the only advantage. In episode thirteen, Ken Farrington appeared as Billy Walker and made the character his own.

During the frenzy of the last few lead-up weeks one decision remained unmade. It is a known fact that two ingredients, at the top and tail of every drama show, cause more trouble than all the rest of the programme put together. These are the title and the curtain line. This time the curtain line was strong enough and inviolable, but the original title was causing a great deal of trouble. I have referred to the programme as *Coronation Street* so far, but that was merely to avoid confusion. As late as the first week of November 1960 we knew the serial as *Florizel Street*, which may cause a few brows to furrow but which is explained by the fact that on Tony Warren's bedroom wall – and he did most of his writing in his bedroom – hung a picture of Prince Charming hacking his way through the enchanted forest to awaken his sleeping princess. And Prince Charming's name was Florizel. Doubts had been cast on this title ever since it had first appeared on the title sheet of Tony's opus, but Tony had fought hard for its retention. As a writer I can well understand his feelings. If you can't christen your own baby who can? However, I must confess that I was among the ranks of doubters, and our doubts were given substance when an actor, during an audition, had to pronounce the name of the street and gave the word a hard 'i' thereby changing it at a stroke into a scented sanitary product.

Tony, quite rightly avoiding other disappointments,

bowed out of the argument and left the field free for Harry Elton, Harry Latham and myself to settle. As one does on these occasions we chickened out. We turned our minds to other things and hoped that the ideal title would appear, miraculously, written in the eastern sky in letters of fire. Unfortunately it didn't and it came as no surprise when, a couple of weeks before our first date of transmission, the order came from above to find a title without further delay. The call had come to Harry Latham from Cecil Bernstein, the younger of the two brothers who had founded the Granada empire and who was the 'grandfather' of the serial from its inception; his death in 1981 was a sad and irreplaceable loss to the programme. Harry Elton, Harry Latham and I took our task very seriously indeed and at seven o'clock the three of us locked ourselves into Harry Latham's office with a couple of bottles of Irish whiskey for company and applied ourselves to our task.

The opening moves were simple and productive. We all agreed that the street had been built around the turn of the century and it was an easy step from this historical point to arrive at two suitable candidates. Had the street gone up in the late 1890s, it could well have been called Jubilee Street to celebrate the Diamond Jubilee of Queen Victoria. Had building started a few years later it could just as easily have been called Coronation Street to celebrate the coming to the throne of Edward VII. We congratulated ourselves on having arrived so quickly at a short list of two and helped ourselves to generous measures of whiskey, not realizing that great anguish lay ahead. As any woman will tell you, it is a grave mistake to arrive at a choice of two. Confronted by a rack full of dresses it's easy enough to choose one, but faced with only two choices there is only one answer to the problem – buy both. In our case this was impossible and the arguments began. For hours we debated the pros and cons of each of our suggested titles without getting any nearer to agreement. The cut and thrust of debate and the vanished contents of the whiskey bottles had taken their toll and we

23

were beginning to feel there was no way out of this impasse when Harry Latham fixed Harry Elton and myself with a schoolmasterly eye and pointed out that as there were three of us and only two candidates, if we were to put the matter to a simple vote we were pretty well bound to reach a decision. A vote was taken and a decision was reached. Thankfully we unlocked the door and went home to our welcoming beds.

The following morning copies of a memorandum from Harry Latham winged their way to every interested recipient in Granada announcing that the new serial was to be known as *Coronation Street*. One of the copies was waiting for me as I arrived and I immediately took it into Harry Elton's office on the sixth floor. He was sitting at his desk reading his copy as I walked in. His head lifted. 'I'm pretty darned sure I voted for Jubilee Street,' he said.

'And I'm pretty darned sure *I* voted for Jubilee Street too,' I added.

And thus it was that our serial came to be known as *Coronation Street*.

In those early years of ITV, once a programme got under way the producer was the undoubted boss, so it could have been that Harry Latham was merely jumping the gun when he decided that nothing as stupidly democratic as a free vote was going to interfere with his choice of title. Democracy was, however, the name of the game as far as other decisions were concerned. One of them was the choice of music.

At that time Granada's 'Music Man' was Eric Spear, a talented musician who wrote most of his incidental themes and signature tunes at his home in Catel, a quiet little village in the centre of the island of Guernsey. Having created, he would fly over to London, gather together a combo of his favourite musicians and record the piece.

He would then fly back as fast as the plane could carry him.

When the time came to think about a signature tune for our new serial, it was decided not to drag Eric Spear up to Manchester but to see what he could make of the first five of Tony Warren's scripts. These were duly sent to him and a couple of weeks later a tape reached us at Granada. On it was the piano version of the proposed music. A covering letter explained the composition of the group he would use, and pointed out that the dominant instrument would be a cornet. A small group of arbitrators met to hear the tape and agreement was both speedy and total. Eric was telephoned and told to get on with it. Off he flew to London, gathered his band of minstrels around him and produced the evocative sounds which still introduce the programme today.

The pieces were knitting together, the jigsaw was almost complete. Denis Parkin, the designer, had submitted his studio plan to Derek Bennett, who was to direct the first two episodes and, the plan having been approved, was now supervising the building and painting of the sets in Granada's vast construction shops. One difficulty arose when the completed sets were erected in Granada's Studio Two and the cameras turned upon them. They looked fine when viewed with the naked eye but the television camera has strange characteristics. Whilst it is no friend of the human face – it can pick out a wrinkle at forty yards – it is exceptionally generous towards inanimate objects. Wall coverings, furniture and the normal trappings of life have a brightness and a glamour in the eyes of the television camera which they certainly don't possess in the eye of the normal beholder. In fact the usual reaction of any studio visitor on being shown the sets of practically any show is 'Oo, isn't it scruffy!' Little do they know that the sets have deliberately been made scruffy to dampen down the glamorizing effect of the camera.

In *Coronation Street*'s case the main offender was the corner shop. Although it had been constructed and decked out with all its paraphernalia as a faithful reproduction of the real thing, the shop and its contents looked far too glossy and Denis Parkin spent many hours covering every surface with a matt grey finish before the set was finally granted the seal of approval.

Although Tony Warren and I were busily occupied at that time, Tony writing the remaining seven episodes of his opening twelve-episode stint and myself following on with episodes thirteen to sixteen, the busiest men were undoubtedly the programme directors. Their casting sessions over and their initial talks with their teams behind them, they were now privately engaged in working out their camera scripts. This is a process where the director, preferably in the peace and quiet of his own home with the telephone off the hook, works out the complicated maze of cast and camera movements. And his job was so much the harder in those early days. Videotape was still in its infancy and although programmes could be recorded there was very little editing. Today a director can constantly stop his recording, put right any errors and, the week after the show has been completed, take fifty pieces of tape into the editing suite and put them all together to make the finished product. But not then.

In the late months of 1960 once you started the show you carried on, come what may, until the end. Not only was this wearing on the nerves but it posed problems of movement. The writer was trained not to give any one character the last speech in one scene and the first speech in the next, for the simple reason that it was physically impossible for him or her to be in two places at more or less the same time. Short buffer scenes were written after, say, character A had left in order to give him time to dash across the studio and take up his position in another set for the beginning of the next scene. This applied too to the cameras, and a studio in the full flow of production with actors and cameras dashing about madly hither and thither was a sight to be seen. You don't get that sort of excitement nowadays. Today the director merely murmurs 'Stop tape!' into his microphone, the entire studio comes to a dignified halt and actors and cameras stroll over to their new positions. Which explains why everything takes twice as long today and causes twice as much trouble.

Casting was now complete and contracts had been exchanged with the lucky twenty-four for the first – and possibly only – thirteen weeks of the new serial. On the morning of Monday, 5 December 1960 the cast of *Coronation Street* gathered en masse for the first time. Under the direction of Derek Bennett rehearsals began in one of the large areas set aside by Granada for that purpose. To produce fifty minutes of drama in a short week's schedule was, and still is, no mean feat and most of the cast knew their lines before they arrived for the first day's dry rehearsal. But the learning of lines was only a small part of the exercise. Characters had to be discussed and formed and it is interesting to note that after all these years those artists who were in the first episode and are with us today still jealously guard the characters they began to create in that December week of 1960. This guardianship applies of course to all our regular artists whenever they came into *Coronation Street* and heaven help any writer or director who tries to foist on to any one of them an action or a line which is obviously 'out of character'. Any hint of that kind of thing and the actor or actress immediately – and quite rightly – jumps to the defence of his or her *alter ego*.

In the middle of each rehearsal week – in our case after lunch each Wednesday – the director would hold what is called a technical or producer's run, to which senior technicians and other interested parties were invited. The pattern began that first week and I went along to the rehearsal room having no idea what I might find. *Coronation Street* has always been a wordy programme and the actors have rarely been given an easy ride as far as the volume of lines was concerned. But this in no way appeared to have bothered our

27

cast. There was an enthusiasm, an excitement about the rehearsal which perhaps should have given a clue as to what lay ahead. Television – even Independent Television – had been going sufficiently long for the honeymoon period to have ended, and most drama rehearsals of that time were rather bored affairs with uninvolved artists sitting in various corners of the studio with their crossword puzzles or knitting. Normally an air of languor hung heavily over the whole proceedings, but not here. Here, in the bare, cold rehearsal room furnished with utility representations of the real thing, exhilaration seemed to set alight the dull December afternoon. Everyone, involved or not, participated in everything. There was an abiding interest not only in one's own role, but in everyone else's. It wasn't to last – nothing does – but there is still, after two decades, more argument and passion generated in the making of *Coronation Street* than in the production of many a new drama programme.

Rehearsal was not the artists' only occupation in that first week. They would find themselves, at any slack moment, kidnapped by a determined wardrobe mistress or an anxious make-up girl eager to practise their various crafts before the production day actually dawned. Make-up was applied, wiped off and applied again, wigs were tried and discarded, moustaches glued to upper lips, and coats, suits, dresses, costumes, shoes and hats moulded onto tired bodies until everyone, particularly the director, was satisfied. On the Thursday afternoon the entire circus moved into Granada's Studio Two and cameramen, sound engineers, lighting supervisors and their electricians, stage hands and all the technical paraphernalia of the electronic miracle joined the fray. Now it was that the cast, for the first time, saw and acted out their parts in 'genuine' surroundings. The shop was no longer the collection of packing cases and planks they had used during rehearsal but as near to the real thing as designers and property men could make. Every tiny ingredient was there. Jars and bottles and boxes and packets, roast meats and cabbages, combs and caramels, cans and confectionery. And every item ready to develop into a potential headache.

In those early days every product on the shelves of our shop or behind the bars of our public house was camouflaged to make it unrecognizable. As the years passed we were to become less careful – at times downright careless – and it was then that trouble loomed. Let us suppose that, instead of every tin of soup on the shelves of our corner shop being a 'Key' product (*Coronation Street*'s own brand name), only the front few tins were camouflaged and the rest were dummies of a branded article obtained from various suppliers. And suppose, too, that the corner shop proprietor had, at one point of the show, when offering a tin of soup to say, 'I know this isn't as good as your usual brand, but I'm afraid it's all I've got.' And, carrying supposition even further, suppose she were, in the excitement of the moment, to fumble behind the first rank on the shelf and say those same words whilst offering to camera a genuine, recognizable tin of soup. It happened to me when I was producing and I spent the best part of the day following our transmission placating an enraged manufacturer.

Nor was it much better if you praised the product. When that happened the complaints were not from the company concerned but from every one of his competitors asking when they were going to get their share of free advertisement. Fortunately today everyone seems to have come to terms with the problem but in those early years, particularly when *Coronation Street* was climbing to the top of the ratings, many a keen commercial eye was thrown in our direction. Behaviour was important, too. It wasn't enough for Florrie Lindley to look like a shopkeeper and Annie Walker to look like a publican's wife, they must act professionally too. I remember once receiving a twelve-page telegram from the General Secretary of the National Association of Small Shopkeepers making that very point. But those problems lay ahead – on Friday, 9 December 1960 all that mattered was that we should launch *Coronation Street* onto the screen.

When, some months previously, *Coronation Street* had been offered to the network, Tyne-Tees Television and ATV Midlands had opted out. Tyne-Tees was to join us three months after the start and ATV Midlands a further three months later. It was then, when we were fully networked, that we first moved to our regular slot at 7.30 pm on Mondays and Wednesdays. For the first six months of *Coronation Street*'s existence, we transmitted the programme live on Friday at 7.00 pm, until 7.30 and after a quarter hour's break recorded the second episode for transmission at 7.00 on the following Monday.

The morning and afternoon of Friday, 9 December were taken up by camera runs and dress rehearsals. After a break for mainly uneaten meals, the cast and technicians regathered in the studio shortly before H-hour and the last few minutes began to tick away. At seven o'clock precisely Eric Spear's music drifted from a host of television receivers, the title of the programme appeared on the screen for the first time, the director cut to the shop interior and Elsie Lappin, the departing shopkeeper, addressed Florrie Lindley, the new arrival, with the words, 'Now next thing you've got to do is get the sign-writer in. That thing above the door will have to be changed.'

I watched the first two episodes in Harry Elton's office with Harry Latham and Tony Warren. We were largely silent and only pretended to relax during the fifteen-minute break which followed the first episode. When the closing music signalled the end of Monday's episode and Harry Elton leaned over and switched off his set, none of us was anxious to come out with a forthright prophecy of success or failure. Generally, we decided, we were pleased. There was a vibrancy, a 'life' in the programme which didn't loom all that large elsewhere in television drama, but was that enough? We knew we were different, but were we different in the right way? And although all of us swore that whatever the Press said about us, it wouldn't have the slightest effect on our thinking, we couldn't wait for the next morning's papers to hit the streets. Somehow we had to celebrate and at the same time to anaesthetize ourselves against the hours of waiting. There was only one thing to do. We all went out and we got drunk.

CHAPTER THREE

'It must be true, Mrs Sharples – it was in this morning's paper.'

Emily Nugent

To say that Press reaction was mixed would be to commit a violent understatement. Comment ranged from the sublime to the gorblimey. Mary Crozier of the *Guardian* said we could run for ever, and loved us passionately until her retirement because we appeared to be proving her right. A colleague in the *Daily Mirror* who intimated that we wouldn't last our thirteen weeks has rarely since said a good word about us, because we had the temerity to prove him wrong. Generally, though, reaction was good. Most of the critics appeared to be intrigued and those who felt they must justify their existence by criticizing something, picked, not always with success, on small points of social behaviour. 'Who,' asked one tabloid writer, 'mends his bicycle in front of the living-room fire in this day and age?' The following week the same paper was forced to print a selection from many dozens of letters it had received from ladies and gentlemen who did that very thing, including one who regularly dismantled his motorbike on the front-room carpet.

Millions of words have been written about *Coronation Street* since those early days, many of them complimentary, but in spite of the constant attentions of the British Press I have found its methods less than enchanting. The strange belief that, with the NUJ card, comes a God-given right to invade the privacy of both people and institutions has never endeared itself to me.

The 'public interest' which the Press proffers so glibly as an excuse is rarely more than their own. I never could and never will understand why it should be in the public interest for newspapers to disclose the plots of television programmes before the viewers can enjoy those programmes on the screen but, despite every plea and blandishment, if a Press man gets hold of a future *Coronation Street* story he prints it. Nothing was calculated to make my temperature soar faster than an irate viewer phoning me in the middle of a busy day and asking me why on earth I had given a particular newspaper the ending of a story which was currently halfway through on the screen. It is doubtful if he would have believed that certain papers had paid informers inside the studios. But they had.

At the beginning of *Coronation Street*, when I wrote and script edited for the programme, I was rarely concerned with Press matters, but from 1962 when I took over as producer and, in later years, executive producer, I found myself deeply involved. *Coronation Street* certainly became a darling of the Press – which doesn't mean it was continually showered with praise. Hitler too was a darling of the British Press. So was Idi Amin. So is anyone who is always good for the odd column, and *Coronation Street* was always that. What one had to realize, I discovered, was that the friendly approach when one was asked for the story wasn't going to count for much when the story actually appeared. In spite of this one couldn't help but admire these jovial hypocrites. Knowing that they had done the dirty on you last week, they were quite capable of coming back with a cheerful 'Hello, Harry!' and yet another request for privileged information. The only answer, I decided at one point, was to treat them like the Gestapo, give one's name, rank and number and leave them to pick the bones out of that. But even then one couldn't win. The astute reporter would make up his own story, based very loosely indeed on fact, print it and invite you to issue a denial. This way he filled twice as much space and so endeared himself to his editor.

My amazement that honest men could do such jobs didn't

prevent me from enjoying a drink with members of the Manchester Television Press Corps. It could in fact be said that, between wars, we were all very pally. Most of them were equipped with a dry humour and generally they were always good for a laugh. And there's no denying they were clever people. John Stevenson of the *Daily Mail* (who became even cleverer when he left journalism and joined the *Coronation Street* scripting team), Ken Irwin and Ken Tossell of the *Daily Mirror*, Gerry Dempsey of the *Express*, Paddy O'Neill of the *Mail* and Keith McDonald of the *Manchester Evening News* were all excellent drinking companions.

My friend Norman Frisby in Granada's Press Office would try to stem my tears by reminding me that any publicity was good publicity, another cliché which I could never accept. It seemed that I was constantly being asked to co-operate but never got any co-operation in return. Two stories help to make this point. A few days before the screening of the 500th episode of the serial, at a time when I was occupying the producer's chair, I received a request from a now-defunct tabloid newspaper for facilities to take a photograph of the entire cast and production team for inclusion in that paper on the day of the anniversary. Because of the short notice this would have meant disturbing rehearsals for a considerable length of time. With the best organization in the world it is difficult to take less than an entire morning or afternoon in setting up a photograph which would have involved the presence in the studio of well over a hundred people. I informed the editor that regretfully I couldn't meet his request and the following day learned to my amazement that he had complained to Granada's management. Apparently I had been accused of being obstructive. In order to show my goodwill I arranged a meeting that day with the picture editor and his reporter. I put all the difficulties in front of him, and reiterated that we could not possibly set up the picture he wanted. However, to cover his disappointment I offered him a *quid pro quo*.

The following week Violet Carson was returning to *Coronation Street* after a long absence and her return was to be something of a surprise. I offered him an exclusive picture and interview with Violet on her return on the understanding that neither picture nor story could be used until the day following her surprise reappearance on the screen. This was agreed and the following week a photographer and, somewhat strangely, a reporter from the parent newspaper appeared to conduct the interview. Again, it was made clear that there was an embargo on the use of the material until after the screen appearance but, in spite of this, picture and story appeared in the parent paper several days before the return of Ena on the screen, thus killing dead any surprise element we might have achieved.

The next example illustrates the general eagerness of the Press to spread alarm and confusion and their reluctance to be deflected, even by common sense, from their chosen path.

One autumn evening in the late 1960s, I was telephoned at home by a highly respected television critic. He had recently given up his staff job for a freelance career but had been asked by his managing editor to write *Coronation Street*'s obituary. It appeared that the said managing editor had noticed that over the past few weeks our ratings had dropped to the bottom half of the Top Ten and, convinced that the end was near, he was making arrangements for the funeral. The critic was not so easily persuaded that the skids were truly under the serial and he was telephoning to have a chat about it. I could have let him go ahead and print but, bearing him no ill will, I pointed out that for the apparently declining weeks in question our competition on BBC-1 had been a first run of *Steptoe and Son* on the Monday night and a rather superior seven-part crime serial on the Wednesdays. It was only natural that our ratings should take a dip, but, as both these highly competitive programmes had finished their runs the week before, I fully expected *Coronation Street* to resume its rightful place at the top of the ratings when they were next published the following Saturday.

He told me that he wouldn't be writing the obituary, thanked me and rang off. The following morning the staff man who had taken his place on the paper telephoned me to say that he had been *told* by the same managing editor that *Coronation Street* was on its last legs etc, etc, and had been *ordered* to write a death bed scene. I supplied him with all the arguments I had given his predecessor, but, alas, he would have none of them. He asked me for a few dying words which I refused to utter and he too rang off. The following Saturday morning, the piece duly appeared in his newspaper. *Coronation Street* was doomed. The recent slump in the ratings was only the start of a long slippery slope from which the serial would never recover. All this would have made tense reading indeed had it not been that in other newspapers that morning the ratings showed that the serial was back to first and second place in the Top Ten, positions it held for many months afterwards.

One more example may help to explain my disaffection with the ladies and gentlemen of the Press. Some years ago the hallowed columns of *Punch* carried a review of *Coronation Street* by a distinguished lady contributor in which the production team was taken to task for bringing a character back from the dead in order to suit our nefarious ends. We were severely chastised for reintroducing the character of Sheila Birtles when it was well known that the girl in question had committed suicide in the programme some years previously. This, the lady columnist implied, was disgraceful behaviour on our part and it would have been, had her facts been right. Unfortunately, unlike some twenty million viewers who were all aware of the truth, the lady word-spinner didn't know that the suicide attempt had been unsuccessful and the character had been restored to full health before leaving the programme. It is bad enough that a writer who is considered an expert in her field and who has access to the columns of such an illustrious weekly should base a review on a mistake which would not have been made by half the population of the British Isles but there is a worse aspect. No one had bothered to check with us before the accusations were printed, and they implied that we were quite capable of treating our viewers as forgetful morons. And that's plain insulting!

Not all journalists of course worked for the printed page. There were many people employed by the various radio services, by the BBC and inside Independent Television. Their methods were roughly the same except that they used a microphone or a tripod leg in the door instead of the foot.

Independent Television, at its inception, had been something of a magnet. Offering as it did high wages, it had attracted people away from the BBC, across the Atlantic and the Indian Oceans from the commercial television systems of the Commonwealth, from the theatre, from the film industry and from the ranks of newspaper journalism. Initially and foreseeably this latter element had drifted into its rightful area of news-gathering and current affairs, but when, a few years later, departmental distinctions became fuzzier round the edges, ex-Pressmen began to drift into other areas of the industry. And not always successfully. Journalism and drama were, I have always considered, an oil and water mix. There were, once again, notable exceptions – Derek Granger, *Coronation Street*'s second producer, had been a drama critic and a distinguished man of the theatre before he joined Granada and was possessed of all the right qualifications, whilst Peter Eckersley of the *Guardian* became a talented scriptwriter, a most efficient producer and a creative Head of Granada's Drama Department – but others lacked the warmth and considerateness required. Perhaps it is wrong to say that they lacked these qualities and more correct that they had deliberately suppressed them in order better to do their previous Press jobs. Whatever the reason, they were uneasy bed fellows when asked to cohabit with the more emotionally motivated artists and writers on their teams.

It may seem that I am matching hypocrisy with hypocrisy if on the one hand I complain about the Press and on the other use its words to my own advantage. Let me therefore make one thing clear. Most of my censure is reserved for the television *reporter* rather than the critic. The reporter it is who not only gives the game away and bends the facts to suit his ends but wastes valuable time in the process, and time has always been at a premium on *Coronation Street*. The critic, on the other hand, has a quite different function. He merely discusses programmes of the previous day or week and, on rare occasions, offers constructive criticism. I say 'on rare occasions' with a deal of sadness as I have always felt that the critic should concern himself more with the creative processes of television than with its subject matter. However – particularly in the Sunday papers – the critics tend to rid themselves of their frustrations by giving at great length their views on drug abuse or teenage violence or parliamentary democracy whilst uttering not a word of comment on the presentation of the programmes under review.

Only on rare occasions do the entire corps of critics devote themselves to *Coronation Street*. Otherwise the individual reviewer will drop in on the programme every two or three years and base his remarks on a single below-par episode out of two hundred good ones, much as Egon Ronay may drop in on a restaurant for an annual check and find he's arrived on the chef's night off, except that Egon Ronay would probably appreciate the situation and go again the following night. However, on anniversaries the programme tends to get the full treatment and it was interesting to read what the critics had to say about the serial on the occasion of its thousandth episode. Here is a selection:

The *Street*'s strength is that starting from an almost photographic realism, it allows itself a fantastic touch from time to time. But always it sticks to some simple moral rules, rules to which a great part of its audience can relate. It shows people themselves, and it takes them out of themselves. Which sounds to me very much like a formula for ever.

BILL GRUNDY – *Spectator*

The serial may have some worth as an entertainment and as a drug for the undecided, lonely and unassured, but it also does harm . . . by perpetuating outdated class distinction and by its protrayal of the grumbling, grudging, unenlightened aspects of Northern life.

Television To-day

Just as the most popular bed-time tales tend to feature children with characteristics suspiciously similar to those of the listener, so the casting of *Coronation Street*'s original characters was quite brilliant.

CHRIS DUNKLEY – *The Times*

. . . any regrets that one may have for never laying eyes on *Coronation Street* (and there are many people who have never seen it) would be felt not through having missed any significant art but through having missed a social phenomenon.

STANLEY REYNOLDS – *The Times*

In a sense, the success of *Coronation Street* reflects fairly enough the success of ITV. It is certain that we would never have had a Northern backstreet serial if Sir Robert Fraser had not thought of the regionalized network and Sidney Bernstein had not believed in Manchester as a real place on the map.

PETER BLACK – *Daily Mail*

39

The Street is either a place you would like to live in, or be glad you got out of. It is intimate, nosey, brutally sharp-spoken, and no one gets away with a thing.

MARY MALONE – *Daily Mirror*

It's all too much. Jammy with action. 'It's life,' according to the executive producer, but life, as anyone in Coronation Street could tell him, is not all jam.

NANCY BANKS-SMITH – *Guardian*

Disapprove of soap opera if you must – but at least take pleasure in the fact that British TV produces the world's best of the genre.

BERNARD DAVIES – *Television Mail*

It has now been going for a decade, though it seems a century: I'll swear it's put 90 years on my life, and I don't even watch it.

Sunday Telegraph

Strange that despite many attempts, no one has produced a middle-class soap opera with anything like the magnetism of the *Street*. A question perhaps of physical and social unity – the terrace and its enforced propinquity?

MAURICE WIGGIN – *Sunday Telegraph*

No bestseller that one knows of has had such a prolific success, except perhaps the Bible. How has it achieved it and what is it that it offers? I confess myself baffled.

T. C. WORSLEY – *Financial Times*

At some time or another over the past twenty years, every critic has both praised and condemned *Coronation Street*. The praise has been, largely, that we kept faith with Tony Warren's initial belief that we should explore life in a Northern working-class street and, in so doing, entertain. The adverse criticism has mainly been that we have failed to meet our obligations as a social documentary.

Other criticisms have been fairer. The programme has softened, it has been said. Characters have become far too mellow, the grittiness of the original stories has been sanded down to a bland smoothness. These comments I will, to a degree, accept but purely as comments, not as strictures. The mere fact that the programme has lasted for twenty years has imposed its own restrictions. What is acceptable in the short term is unbearable in the long. Can anyone imagine Alf Garnett twice a week for twenty years? Can anyone exist on a diet of jam? (Any regular viewer could tell Nancy Banks-Smith of the *Guardian* that *Coronation Street* has had its share of bitter aloes.) Or can anyone keep body and soul together solely on vinegar? For these reasons the serial has changed. Ena Sharples *has* softened but in the way that many women soften over twenty years. She is less disturbed now by death, more angered by rising prices. Life's big worries have gone – she has seen them for what they are – but life's pinpricks continue to multiply.

As a footnote to this chapter on *Coronation Street* and the Press I would like to make it quite clear that my antipathy is based on the misdeeds of a few of its members. Other areas of the Fourth Estate are, I am sure, inhabited by delightful human beings. Gardening correspondents are, to take an example, the salt of the earth whilst book reviewers will always be, to a person, wonderful, wonderful people.

CHAPTER FOUR

'I went to stay wi' me great-niece in Birmingham last
back end. They couldn't understand owt I said.'

Albert Tatlock

If the Press had mixed feelings about the advent of this
strange newcomer, the viewing public accepted *Coronation
Street* from the outset. Admittedly it was like-at-first-sight
rather than love, but those of us with a stake in the programme were well pleased with that. One of the battles we
had fought and won in those pre-transmission months had
been over dialect. Harry Latham, Tony Warren and I had
battled against any watering down of the south-east
Lancashire idiom with which the dialogue was sprinkled.
No concessions, we argued, could be made to the inhabitants of Scotland or Wales, East Anglia or the New
Forest. Most of the inhabitants of those areas were quite
familiar with the idiom of the American prairie through
long exposure to Westerns which themselves had conceded
nothing to British audiences. But winning the battle was
one thing, finding out if our cause had been a just one was
another and we waited with some trepidation to see what
happened. Would the people of Norwich, totally at sea
with what our characters were talking about, switch us
off *en masse*? Would the Cornish fisherman imagine that he
had picked up some foreign station and re-adjust his
aerial? Happily neither of these things came to pass.
After a few weeks we found that allegiance to our programme had grown in the strangest parts of Britain. Whether
or not these non-Northerners considered our characters to
be queer fish and set aside the two *Coronation Street* days
for visits to the aquarium or whether they were genuinely
interested and entertained by these strange British cousins

we were never quite sure. All we knew was that they watched us in great numbers and they continue to watch us.

The greatest test, however, lay close to home. If the Lancastrians gave us the thumbs down then we had truly failed and the viewing figures we awaited with the most eagerness were those of Granada's own region. We needn't have worried. Apart from the odd moan that we were showing the North of England in a bad light (about which more later) the streets of the industrial North were solidly behind us.

The question I am most asked is to what do I attribute the serial's success. Ask fifty people, all as involved with the programme as myself, and you will receive fifty different answers but mine has always been unequivocal. During the first two or three years of its existence, commercial television offered no more points of identification to the great mass of their audience than did the BBC. Admittedly the independent companies didn't force their newsreaders into evening dress but the entertainment they offered was largely escapist and only in the dourest of documentaries did the cameras move into the teeming back streets of the industrial cities.

This is as good a place as any to explain my definition of a phrase which will be used again and again in these chapters: 'working class'. I have always understood the phrase to cover that multitude of employees who, without responsibility, perform the many boring, difficult and laborious tasks which guarantee the survival of the economy. And, prior to *Coronation Street*, when these same people after a long, boring and laborious day returned to their firesides and the television set, they could watch until the dot disappeared into the blackness of the screen but they would never find themselves mirrored there. And then, one December night in 1960, everything changed. Not only was his pub to be seen, but that old biddy whose curtains were forever twitching, and the gay widow from number eleven that he had had his eye on for years, and Harry the bus inspector, who was having trouble with his kid, and the corner shop that had just been done for selling firelighters. It was a revolution. No longer did the world consist of hospitals and police stations and courtrooms; no longer was it populated solely by members of 'the other half'. The great mass of people had been acknowledged and, not only that, they had shown themselves to be a dramatic force.

This is not to say that *Coronation Street* was the first element in the entertainment industry to throw the spotlight on to working people. There had been films and stage plays which had exploited their humour and their problems but it must be remembered that in the late 1950s the cinema was in decline and the theatre was the province of a very small proportion of the population. For the vast majority the first introduction to drama came from the gleaming eye in the corner of the sitting-room. For the first time, too, four-fifths of the population was hearing its everyday problems aired in popular discussion. And I mean *everyday* problems. Not death and divorce, murder and mayhem but the very minutiae of life. How could Ken Barlow take his 'posh' girlfriend to tea at the Imperial Hotel knowing that his mother washed dishes in the kitchens there? Was Florrie Lindley, the new incumbent at the corner shop, strong enough to resist her formidable neighbours' requests for 'tick'? Would Lucille Hewitt pass her eleven-plus? These were questions of an order never previously explored in television drama. These were the true trivia of life. Not 'trivialities' (a debasement of the word) but trivia. Matters of family and individual importance were discussed by the Roman citizenry at the 'trivium' – the meeting of the three ways – and are just as absorbing and as problematical today as they were then. It was the serial's involvement with these themes, its concentration on the everyday worries and the minor ambitions of the ordinary person, that, I am convinced, first built the programme's popularity and laid the foundations of a viewer-loyalty quite unique in entertainment history.

There was another side to the coin. The serial, concentrating as it did on the working class, was in some areas considered not quite 'the thing', and many a secret middle-class viewer would deny it several times before cock crow. I frequently met people in pubs who, when it was explained to them by our mutual aquaintances that I worked in television, would first say: 'Could you come and have a look at my set? I can't get a decent picture on BBC-2' and then, when it was further explained that I was nothing so exalted as an engineer but merely wrote scripts for *Coronation Street*, would smile at me, their eyes dimmed with pity, and say: 'Do you know I have never seen it?' Which was fair enough. Only half the viewing population *did* see it with any regularity but if these strange people hadn't ever seen it, how did they come to know who had written that anonymous letter to Elsie Tanner? Why were they so concerned about Ena's health? The difference, I discovered, between the original denial and the later absorbing interest was usually three large scotches. Perhaps I shouldn't have been so surprised. Television had, by that time, taken the place of sex as the British primary matter of conscience, and the grim warnings against its addiction were much the same – too much of it was bad for you and it should never be indulged in during the hours of daylight.

History, I suppose, was merely repeating itself, and we were suffering the same treatment at the hands of the hypocritical as had literature in pre-television days. Those who watched *Coronation Street* only behind closed curtains and would die rather than admit it were the TV equivalent of those ladies and gentlemen who carried around their James Bond novels in *War and Peace* dust covers, and who only admitted to watching documentaries and the odd play. If memory serves me right I never met a single person in those early days who didn't *always* watch *Panorama*. I couldn't understand why *Panorama* wasn't top of the ratings every week.

Things are better now. People are less snobbish about

their viewing habits. But in those days, just embarking on a new adventure, it hurt a little. Which made it doubly pleasing when, in the show's early days, I was introduced to a chap who looked at me reverently, asked for my autograph (for his little girl, of course) and suggested that I might like to come along and 'talk to his lot'. I said I would be delighted, a date was fixed and I hurried home to plan my lecture. Obviously this was a serious exercise and I applied myself seriously to the task. The result was a most erudite talk full of sociolinguistic and sociometric references. Leaning heavily of course for its conclusions on environmental studies etc., etc.

On the appointed evening I took myself and my much-rehearsed speech to that cold little brown-painted room with the hard wooden seats where all such affairs appear to be held and was heard in respectful silence by a small but obviously highly intelligent audience. At the end a charming lady rose to her feet, thanked me most profusely and asked if she might put a question. I concurred graciously.

'Tell me, Mr Kershaw,' she said, 'does Bobby the cat really belong to the lady who plays Minnie Caldwell?'

My next talk corrected all my previous mistakes. It was a string of gossipy items about cats and Elsie Tanner's love life and where did Violet Carson have her hair done, and it was listened to avidly with polite bursts of laughter at just the right moments. And at the end a charming lady rose to her feet, thanked me profusely and asked how I viewed *Coronation Street* sociolinguistically.

It was at that point that I realized that different people wished to know different things and from then on I didn't deliver lectures, I answered questions. But even this had its disadvantages and its dangers. I was once asked to fill one of the spots in a season of midday talks in Manchester's Library Theatre. People with nothing better to do during their lunch break simply wandered in, sat down and listened to whoever happened to be the dish of the day. The lectures were well publicized and I found myself facing a mixed but uniformly fierce-looking audience of about a hundred.

As was then my wont I treated them to a five- or six-minute introductory chat and then invited them to ask away. I have never known there to be a shortage of questions and this was no exception. The lunch hour bowled merrily along until one gentleman rose to his feet, fixed me with a sardonic eye and asked 'Mr Kershaw, are you honestly telling us that *Coronation Street* is real?' No, I wasn't, I explained. The stories told within the serial were, I suggested, real enough; what was unreal was the sheer amount of dramatic event in that one street. What we had in fact done was to take the dramatic happenings of a hundred streets and encapsulate them into one. To that extent our street was unreal. Life in most streets of our type was ninety per cent sheer unadulterated boredom and although one or two viewers may complain that that in fact was what we were giving them, we certainly hadn't set out to do so. To have shown the real thing in Andy Warhol style with Stan Ogden picking his teeth in front of the television set for the full half hour might have appealed to the odd aesthete but was no way to hold a mass audience.

The questioner, apparently satisfied, sat down and we all carried on. It wasn't until the following morning that I realized a very simple truth. If a housewife or a bank clerk or a girl from the Burnley Building Society can wander into the Library Theatre during his or her lunch hour then so can a reporter from the *Daily Telegraph*. And one had. There it was, as large as life, a half column headed 'CORONATION STREET UNREAL,' SAYS PRODUCER. I got a few hard looks from the management during the next two or three days. Not that the hard looks altered my thinking. I still stand by what I had said about the 'reality' of *Coronation Street* and I refuse to subscribe to the widely held belief that many viewers believe our fantasy to be total truth. As my mother whispered so often in the darkened cinema, 'It's only a story,' and, whilst accepting this, millions of viewers are willing to suspend their disbelief in order to heighten the entertainment value. What these viewers *do* feel – and this we take as a compliment – is that our characters and situations are firmly based on the reality they know. Our people are like their people, our problems are of a size with theirs and because of this they will describe *Coronation Street* as real without necessarily believing that were they to visit Manchester on a day trip and walk the streets they would bump into Albert Tatlock going for his pension.

Not all our viewers were from the terraced streets of Britain. The programme, we soon found, had a high nostalgic value and the large part of the population who were only one or at most two generations removed from these Edwardian streets still held the folk memory of life at that level. 'My mother used to live in a street just like *Coronation Street* and it's exactly the way she described it' was a recurring comment.

Diametrically opposed to those too snobbish to admit an addiction to the serial were those who made it a cult. These were the amateur sociologists who saw in *Coronation Street* something which no one had ever put in. The programme was likened to the works of Dickens, even Shakespeare. This led to a great deal of unfair criticism. Whilst one high-toned weekly would extol our social virtues in a learned article another would take issue and condemn the programme for failing to be a useful social documentary – something we never set out to be in the first place. Let Tony Warren explain with the opening words of his original brief. 'A fascinating freemasonry, a volume of unwritten rules. These are the driving forces behind a working-class street in the North of England. Florizel Street sets out to explore these values and in doing so, to entertain.'

The name has changed but the intentions remain to this day.

CHAPTER FIVE

'If money's the root of all evil I must be a flamin' saint!'

Hilda Ogden

Plutocrat to pauper, money is a subject of abiding interest. The questions are constantly being asked: 'How much does *Coronation Street* cost?' 'What do the actors get a week?' 'Is Tony Warren a millionaire?' There is little point in answering the first two questions directly as, in these inflationary days, any figures I gave would be out of date long before this book went into print. But if I offer no figures I *can* offer related words.

In the late 1950s, as has already been said, what mattered most was the making of programmes and not the money those programmes cost, which is not to say that there was a bottomless pit of wealth into which any producer simply dipped in order to satisfy his whims. What I do mean is that in those days, time spent discussing programmes as against the money they cost was in the ratio of about five to one. Nowadays the ratio appears to be three to two in favour of money.

Each producer was given what was known as a development budget which allowed him to build a springboard for his programme. With this money he could pay the expenses of artists who attend auditions. He could keep the writer – and the writer's bank manager – happy with an advance or two. That done, and the programme a firm project, he was required to write a budget for the programme itself. In the case of a serial this would cover several months ahead – say three or six – and in this instance as the programme was only originally scheduled for thirteen weeks that was the extent of the budget period. The budget

49

listed weekly costs – for casting, writers' fees, properties, scenery, wardrobe and make-up charges, the use of film if any, and other related services. The natural instinct is for a producer to go for as much as he can get, but Harry Latham was a man of the theatre and like all men of the theatre he knew that money didn't grow on trees. He also knew that in television particularly money only bought some of life's goodies. The rest were achieved by perseverance and an eye for talent.

So it was that the budget when it finally took shape was not modest, perhaps, which might imply a certain lack of faith in the programme's potential, but sensible. Sensible in that at the start of casting – the biggest single expense on most drama programmes – the expensive, well-known stars of the day were passed by and Granada's two casting directors, Margaret Morris and Josie Scott, shopped around amongst members of Equity, which as anyone in entertainment knows is the world's biggest bargain basement for talent. This vast pool of 'resting' actors and actresses has been formed not through any lack of ability but purely from a shortage of opportunity. At any given moment the vast majority of registered artists in Britain are out of work, a situation due entirely to the fact that once an individual decides that he or she wants to be an actor nothing on God's earth will stop the process, even though one's average year might be nine months serving in a snack bar, two months on starvation wages in repertory and a couple of walk-on parts at Yorkshire Television. And yet in spite of – or perhaps because of – this gloomy outlook, Britain possesses a reservoir of acting ability which is the envy of the world. If competition really does sharpen the skills then this is hardly surprising. Nor is it surprising that, as mentioned in an earlier chapter, there was so much enthusiasm from the artists at the beginning of *Coronation Street*. A thirteen-week engagement, even though broken by an option in the middle, was the stuff as dreams are made on. Not that the fees were astronomic but any television fee made theatre wages look paltry and short-term security was better than no security at all.

The contract system, which was to continue after it became obvious that the show was a 'runner', turned out to be a blessing for all concerned. When, in November 1961, Equity began its seven-month strike against the independent companies, thirteen of the original cast remained under long-term contract. Under the terms of these contracts they were allowed to work throughout the strike and save the programme from what could then have been a death blow. No one knows what might have happened if *Coronation Street*, then less than a year old and just beginning to rise to the top of the ratings, had been taken off the air for over six months. Because of Granada's faith in a deserving band of artists we were, happily, never to find out.

Money is a subject of particular interest to those who don't have great quantities of their own, and the average filmgoer, televiewer and newspaper reader will always be intrigued by Robert Redford's efforts to steal a fortune, Hilda Ogden's modest success at bingo and how this or that lowly-born Cabinet Minister comes to live in such high style. Millions of words are written about the commodity, most of them highly exaggerated. I remember Vince Powell and the late and sorely-missed Harry Driver, the comedy writers, confiding to me in their early days on *Coronation Street* that they had been interviewed by a reporter from a popular national daily. He had asked amongst other things how much they were earning a year but of course they hadn't told him. When he had mumbled something about 'suppose I say six thousand a year each?' they had smiled and given him the old 'no comment'. The following morning, in the middle of a rather nice interview piece, it was noted that neither writer had denied earning six thousand a year. Which in itself was true, but which didn't make the boys' tasks any easier when it came to convincing their respective wives that they earned nothing like that amount. And if that was difficult it was impossible to convince the newspaper reading public. Popular misapprehensions about other people's money are easily spawned, not so easily destroyed. And *Coronation Street* has not escaped these myths.

No one has epitomized glamour in the British mind more than the Hollywood superstar and it was natural that when television became part and parcel of British life its heroes and heroines should be compared in many respects to the celluloid greats of yesteryear, the gods and goddesses who rode in gold-plated limousines, quite often with a live cheetah on the back seat, bathed in pink champagne and spent most of their off-screen time having juicy affairs with each other. Let me say now categorically that I do not know a single actor or actress in Britain who owns a gold-plated car or a cheetah or who bathes in anything other than honest-to-God water. There may be some but if there are I don't know them. Not that my knowledge has deterred the man in the street from expecting this kind of life style from the stars of television, and I have the greatest sympathy with any artist who earns less than the gentleman in the machine room at *The Times* and yet is expected to live in the life style of Caesar or Cleopatra. The vast majority of the cast seem to have come to terms with this strange situation but in those early days, with praise and adulation all around them, life must have been very difficult.

The question of artists' fees on *Coronation Street* was a vexed one. Had every artist been paid a Hollywood star salary the show would have priced itself off the air within a matter of weeks. Nor could Granada single out one or two for extra-special treatment and ignore the rest, and they were quite right in taking this stand. *Coronation Street*, which has had problems enough, would have been made even more difficult to produce had we operated a star system. As it was, everyone in the contract cast was treated more or less the same – there were differentials but only fairly modest ones – and this egalitarian society was one which I and many other producers sought to sustain. There were, however, other areas where the individual rose above the ruck and could indeed have been treated far more generously than his colleagues. It is fair to say, for instance, that had Tony Warren sold an idea for a twice-weekly serial to an American network and the programme had still been high in the ratings after a continuous twenty-year run, he would by now have been dabbling his toes in the second best swimming pool of his Bel Air mansion and wondering where to buy his next apartment house. Suffice it to say that he isn't.

In Britain only the tycoon makes millions from television but that is not to say that we do not all have blessings to count. I, as a writer, cannot translate my scripts onto the television screen single handed. Nor as an author could I – and still make a profit – publish my books myself. Why should I not then be thankful to those visionary gamblers who built up Independent Television, who provided the studios with their vastly complicated and highly expensive hardware and employed, at no small cost, the technical and artistic help which would translate the words of a script and turn them into a television talking picture? Good luck, then, to the companies which give me the opportunity to assist in making their high profits but let them remember that they are members of the talent exchange and talent being the commodity with the world's greatest mark-up they should distribute those profits a little more fairly to those most responsible for them. May I suggest a starting point – the artists and writers who are the true milch cows of the industry?

One final word. This is a book which primarily concerns one programme. When Sidney Bernstein won the contract for the North-West he created a unit based in and responsible to that region. I am sure that from the start, like every other sincere contractor dedicated to the furtherance of his own region, he must have dreamed of the opportunity to produce a highly successful, highly profitable and long-running programme about and largely created by men and women of that region. It was Tony Warren who made Granada's dream come true. Not only has *Coronation Street* supplied an hour of top-rating entertainment every week for the past two decades, it has allowed Granada to experiment in other areas, secure in the knowledge that they are meeting their responsibilities to their chosen territory.

CHAPTER SIX

'I could do wi' bosses if they didn't chuck their weight about so much.'

Eddie Yeats

There is no all-purpose definition of a television producer. He can play any one of a dozen parts depending upon the programme he is producing. He may fulfil a technical, a creative or an executive role; he may be a director/producer who relies on his script editor for a smooth flow of written material; he may be a writer/producer who, to avoid unnecessary clashes, takes on the duties of script editor himself. He (and I apologize for the pronoun – there are numerous talented women producers) may come from a variety of backgrounds. I have mentioned ex-directors and ex-writers but *Coronation Street* has flourished under the reign of producers who came from casting departments, from behind television cameras and from the worlds of research and current affairs. All have brought their individual slant to the programme but all have recognized and kept faith with the programme's fundamental premise.

Comment has already been made about the programme's first producer, Harry (Stuart) Latham. He was the innovator, the style-setter, the man who worked out the nuts and bolts of the programme and made it into a practical week by week proposition. This was by no means as easy as it may sound. Granada had not previously entered the field of the twice-weekly serial and a programme of this nature makes so many recurring demands on a studio's facilities that it could not be treated in the same way as, say, a one-off play or a short drama series. Admittedly *Coronation Street* was, initially, only booked for a thirteen-week run but it soon became evident that this was to be extended and it was at this time that Harry Latham began to consolidate the programme's position inside Granada.

Most of his time was spent discussing the programme's peculiarities with his directors, senior technicians and the Heads of Services involved. He explained that the programme would make differing demands upon different departments. It would not, after the initial flurry of activity, be particularly burdensome on the design department. Once the regular sets had been built, painted and stored away new sets would be introduced only rarely. The problem here became one of storage of the many stock sets demanded by the show rather than one of continuing work. Other services, such as make-up, were to be harder hit. After the show became fully networked and transmissions moved to Monday and Wednesday, both programmes were recorded at the end of the previous week, the first on the Thursday afternoon, the second on the Friday afternoon. This meant that for those two days the make-up department was invaded by a large *Coronation Street* cast and special arrangements had to be made. All these and the multitude of other problems had to be solved during Harry Latham's occupancy of the producer's chair and, quite apart from the many battles he fought and won over the 'tone' of the programme, he also drew up, with the help of his directors, a blue print for production which remains a guide to this day.

Harry Latham left the programme to move onto other things in the late summer of 1961 and was succeeded, rather surprisingly, by Derek Granger. Rather surprisingly, that is, to those who did not realize that Derek had a great affection for the programme. Previously he had been active in what were supposed to be Granada's more prestigious areas and no one at that time thought that *Coronation Street* ranked as a classic. However, Derek did have this genuine affection for the programme and he brought it with him when he moved into the producer's office. A man of tremendous enthusiasm and energy, he worked us all under the table and we were fortunate that he was producing when Equity called their strike in November 1961. As I've noted, long-term contracts were allowed to be honoured and we were left with thirteen regular characters. This may seem ample for the telling of our stories but when one considers that *Coronation Street*'s average cast was twenty-five it will be realized that to operate with only thirteen was more than a mere restriction. There were of course stories operating at that time which had to be drastically altered in mid-stream. Elsie Tanner was in the middle of a torrid affair with Bill Gregory, a naval petty officer played by Jack Watson and although Pat Phoenix was one of our thirteen contract artists and could stay with us, Jack Watson was forced to leave the programme when the strike began in early November. This was a time for contrivance. I remember writing a scene where Elsie, in a phone box, talked to her lover. She had just received an anonymous letter pointing out that her association with him could affect the outcome of her pending divorce and, over the phone, she told the unseen, strike-bound Jack Watson that he had 'better keep out of the way until the trouble blew over'. Which was a piece of double talk if ever there was one.

For a while, whipped on by Derek Granger's enthusiasm, we coped with the strike remarkably well. We played scenes where Len Fairclough and Harry Hewitt sat at a corner table of a strange pub commenting on their noisy but unseen fellow customers. Harry Hewitt was forever shouting upstairs to his strike-bound daughter, Lucille, that she would be late for school. On several occasions we heard her feet pattering down the stairs and the front door slamming but her physical presence was denied to us for the full seven months of the strike.

Our street scenes were largely augmented by child actors. Equity had no complaints when we used children to deliver papers but when we turned them into milkmen and postmen they quite rightly complained, and we stopped the practice. It was then that Derek Granger turned to the inhabitants of Belle Vue, the local zoo. We had chimpanzees and performing seals and a wide variety of God's creatures all helping to fill the spaces left by the striking human beings.

It was during Derek's stewardship that the programme first began to climb into the Top Ten. ITV was maintaining a full service despite the strike but the absence of artists meant, of course, that many of the public's favourite drama programmes were off the air. This probably helped to improve the *Street*'s viewing figures but the shortage of popular entertainment on the ITV channel was by no means the only reason for the show's continuing success. Derek Granger was a perfectionist in everything he did and every thread in the storyline and every word in the finished script were subjected to intense scrutiny before they were passed for consumption. The shortage of humans and the influx of animals led, naturally, to lighter stories but Derek insisted quite rightly that this was no excuse for a slapdash approach. It was he who first propounded a theory which I still hold to be true – that the battle for improved standards would be fought on the field of the mass audience. There is little point in teaching in an empty classroom, nor much joy in preaching to the converted. The great bulk of the television audience were having their first taste of drama through the cathode ray tube and there was a responsibility on the providers of that drama to give the viewers, within the terms of reference of the programme, the best of acting, of writing and of production. It didn't always work out of course – as has been said before, five days is little time to produce fifty minutes of television drama – but there was nothing wrong with trying.

Derek Granger moved from *Coronation Street* shortly before the strike finished in May 1962 and I succeeded him as producer. Some months previously Denis Forman had asked me if I would like to produce one of Granada's drama series *Family Solicitor* but I had declined the offer.

I didn't know much about the programme or the people who were making it and I felt it might be unfair both to the company and to myself if I were to endeavour to find out whilst, at the same time, I was learning the intricacies of production. When, however, the same Denis Forman asked me if I would produce *Coronation Street*, my answer was different. This was a show I knew all about and all I had to concern myself with were the details of the producer's job.

I was happy to carry on in the same vein as my predecessors. Comedy had always played a large part in our scripts and I certainly wasn't about to change that. In fact I saw it as a fact of life that in the real world smiles were much more plentiful than tears. Walk down Manchester's Deansgate on any day and you will see the proof of that statement. Here again Tony Warren had served us well. All our characters were capable of making an audience laugh as well as cry, and the writers were encouraged to put the same mixture into their work.

There was an undoubted thrill in seeing my name on the screen as *Coronation Street*'s producer. Credits (the names you see before and after the production) were always hard to come by at Granada. In the company's early days I am sure that Sidney Bernstein would have been happier had the only credit at the end of each of his shows been the simple Granada caption. He saw us all as members of the family which would have been fine had we stood to inherit the millions but we didn't, so we all wanted credits instead.

Coronation Street had, for me, been a particularly tough nut to crack. At the beginning of the show when I was script editing I was totally responsible for all the stories that were told on the screen, I hired and fired the writers and edited their scripts but, unless I wrote the episode myself, I received no visible credit for my work. The reason given for this by the then Head of the Story Department was that the simple title of script editor did not fully cover the duties I was performing and would therefore be inadequate. Until we could think of a suitable title I was asked to do without and this I did until, in the middle of one night, my wife, who was as frustrated as I was over the missing credit, sprang bolt upright in bed and shouted the magic words 'serial editor!' It was a message from heaven. The following day I put this suggested title to the Story Department and received immediate approval. The following week I became television's first 'serial editor'. Today we have reverted to script editor and no one has noticed the difference.

Producing *Coronation Street* was a lonely job. In those days the management left producers very much to their own devices and put a great deal of power in their hands. They were responsible for any decisions which did not infringe company policy, and this covered a wide area. Not least it involved helping to solve the personal problems of a large cast, and as actors tend by their very nature to have rather more personal problems than the average man or woman this aspect took no little part of the producer's time. But more about that in later pages. In the main the producer concerned himself with the continuing production of the programme. This itself can be strain enough. A long-running serial – and in 1962 *Coronation Street*'s future stretched into infinity – brings its own unique problem to the people who run it. Every week is conservation week. One must always be conscious that a future lies ahead and one has to be very careful to ensure that before cutting a branch from the tree, the life of the tree itself is not endangered. Stories, too, were hard to come by and although we prided ourselves that each episode contained more incident than in the average serial it would have been stupid to play out our stories before we had extracted all the entertainment from them. Add to these considerations the fact that the programme was under constant pressure from outside, that every advertising agency was trying to get their products mentioned *inside* the programme rather than during the commercial breaks, that the Independent Television Authority was watching us like a hawk and that half the population of the British Isles was ready to pounce on us if we made a mistake, and it will be appreciated that no *Coronation Street* producer was looking out for a spare-time job.

On one front, however, the producer's life was serene. Not only had Granada's management given him the power but they had allowed him to use it. Interference was a rare event and I can remember only one occasion where a decision of mine was overruled. Adele Rose, one of our original script writers, had written a scene in which one character belittled a market stall. She had searched her imagination for a suitable nickname for the stall in question, and it was not until the programme had been transmitted that we were told, rather forcibly, by the proprietor of a Northern emporium that the nickname was widely applied to his own store. He asked for an apology to be made on the screen and I refused. Although we were completely innocent of any attempt to libel the man's good name the matter reached solicitor level and the company lawyers decided that an apology should be made. I probably took the decision far more seriously than I should but it seemed to me at the time that a black mark had been placed on the programme's record and we were just as proud of our good name as the offended store owner was of his.

The company's willingness to let producers get on with the job was, as we soon discovered, a two-edged blade. There was no doubt in my mind that it was the right attitude for the management to take but on some occasions the producer was left to make the most agonizing decisions alone and on others he or she made decisions which the company would dearly love to have reversed. But having committed themselves they gritted their teeth and kept out of the picture. Examples of both these eventualities arose during the terms of office of *Coronation Street*'s next two producers.

After over a year in the *Coronation Street* chair I had asked for a change and in the late summer of 1963 I was relieved by Margaret Morris, the serial's first woman producer and the lady who, as a senior casting director, had gathered together our original cast. This appointment kept faith with Granada's wish to keep producers within the family – not Granada's greater family but from the ranks of those who had previously contributed to the serial in some other office. In order to smooth the takeover I had agreed to act as an unaccredited script editor whilst becoming a member of the scriptwriting team. This suited my book. Writing was my first love and after a year without it I was beginning to feel hungry for more happy hours at the typewriter. The arrangement worked well. Margaret Morris had an excellent grasp of all the necessities of production and the programme progressed smoothly until the 'Sheila Birtles' incident reared its head. We were coming to the end of a sad, romantic story involving Sheila and Neil Crossley a 'smoothie' who had led her up the garden path. He deserted her and Sheila decided to take her own life.

It was during the filming of these 'suicide' episodes that the Press got to hear of our intentions. We weren't totally surprised. We had known for some time that somewhere in our organization we were harbouring a 'mole' who was paid to give information to the other side. The story hit the papers after we had made the episode in question but before it could be shown. According to the Press (the story had been started by one tabloid daily but was rapidly taken up by the rest) we had recorded some horrifying scenes which should not reach the screen. Quotes had been obtained from a high official in the Manchester Coroner's office which vilified us for treating suicide 'in this way'. How these people knew which way we were treating suicide remains a mystery. No one from the Coroner's office nor indeed from any of the papers concerned was present during the filming. I was and I can say now that it was the most deterrent piece of television I had seen at that time. Maybe it was too harrowing for many viewers but this would have been a matter for the Archbishop of Canterbury and not for a member of a Coroner's office who should have been glad that we were showing suicide to be such a messy business. Pressure however was mounting. The Independent Television Authority was forced to take a hand and recommendations were made that the offending scene should not be shown. Margaret Morris found herself in the middle of this controversy and although she stuck to her guns until the last moment, sheer weight of opposition forced her in the end to give way. The scenes of Sheila's suicide were never shown and remain on the cutting-room floor.

Throughout this controversy Margaret Morris was left to determine the right course of action and it was quite correct that she should do so. As producer she knew not only the pros and cons of the argument but also the consequences of any decision she might make.

Margaret finished her stint on the serial in early 1964. I had been looking around for a new vehicle to produce, merely as a change from *Coronation Street* and in the previous November Denis Forman called me to his office and asked if I would take over a venture which was at that time in mid-preparation. A freelance producer had brought an idea which Granada had accepted and he had progressed as far as collecting thirteen scripts when he received an offer he couldn't very well refuse from the BBC. Granada released him on his request and this was the project which I was asked to continue. It was called *Railway Police* and when I read the scripts I must confess that my heart sank. It contained all the usual ingredients of the cops and robbers series – a sort of *Z Cars* on the Iron Way – and was not the sort of thing I was either looking for or good at. I went to Denis Forman and told him of my worries, not the least of which was that thirteen scripts would need to be jettisoned. He gulped a little at that one but asked me what I would like to do. I wasn't quite sure and we chatted over the subject. I suggested that we might well explore the world of crime from the other side and look at the stresses and strains of criminal life rather than its glorification, which had been fashionable in the recent past.

Forman agreed, suggested the title of *The Villains* and then dropped his bombshell. It was now the second week in November and rehearsals were to start at the beginning of the second week of January. This left me two months in which to create my team and find scripts. Nowadays no producer would dream of accepting such an assignment but in those days we were all slightly mad and excitement was still the name of the game. Suffice to say that we made our deadlines and the programme became a minor success. It was during my involvement with *The Villains* that the next *Coronation Street* takeover took place. Margaret Morris's successor was Tim Aspinall, an experienced writer and script editor. In no time at all Tim was in deep trouble. He had been told, as had his predecessors, that as producer total responsibility was solely his and it was one of Tim's earliest decisions that caused *Coronation Street*'s most furious fluttering in the dovecotes. He decided to kill off Martha Longhurst.

Ena, Minnie and Martha, the formidable triumvirate of the Rovers Snug, were one of *Coronation Street*'s most popular ingredients and when the word leaked that one of them was to die the Press had a field day. No doubt Tim Aspinall felt that by such action he would bring the programme a great deal of publicity and in this he certainly succeeded. However I do feel – and this is only a personal opinion – that he broke the rule of conservation. By killing an established character he doubtlessly gave us a few episodes of high drama and created a talking-point in the factories and launderettes which boosted our viewing figures for a period, but when the dust settled we were simply left with a *Coronation Street* without Martha Longhurst. The trio had been reduced to a rather sad duet and there is little doubt that by that one action many future stories were denied us. What is interesting is that as far as I know, at no time did Granada's management seek to change Tim Aspinall's mind. And very soon they reaped the benefit. Give a producer freedom and he will make mistakes, but he will also be creative.

Within a few weeks of Martha Longhurst's departure, a new family, the creation of Tim Aspinall, appeared on the screen. Not only was he largely responsible for their characterizations but for their casting, and there is little doubt that, although the new family were low key for a little while, he had brought to the programme the best dramatic inventions since the original characters were conceived by Tony Warren. Some you win and some you lose and I would far rather remember Tim Aspinall not as the man who killed off Martha Longhurst, but as the man who gave birth to Hilda, Stan and Irma Ogden.

The end of my stint on *The Villains* coincided with Tim Aspinall's expressed wish to move on to other things and I was asked if I would return to *Coronation Street* as producer. During my talks with the management it was mutually agreed that the programme had now grown to such a size that it warranted the appointment of an executive producer. Normally only departments (Drama, Current Affairs, etc.) demand the presence of an executive producer but by this time – we were in the mid 1960s – *Coronation Street* had assumed the proportions of an empire. On the one hand the mechanics of production had grown more complex thus giving us less spare time, on the other, demands on the programme, both collective and individual, were increasing rapidly. Could Violet Carson please go to Buckingham Palace to collect her OBE? Would it be possible for Pat Phoenix to be on the Miss World panel? Could we produce a *Coronation Street* sketch for a Royal Gala Performance? How about bringing some of the cast out to Australia? And so the demands continued not only to take time in their execution but in their planning and for this reason it was decided that the show should have a producer to look after the day-to-day production of the programme and an executive producer to handle all the extra-mural matters, to make decisions normally made by members of the Board and to concern himself with the long-term future of the serial.

This system worked happily enough. As executive producer I had a variety of friendly and efficient producers over the years. They included the late Richard Doubleday who, as a freelance director had endeared himself to the cast and made himself an obvious choice for the producer's chair. Following Richard came a succession of writer/producers – Jack Rosenthal, John Finch and Peter Eckersley. All of them brought their own individual fortes to the show. Jack Rosenthal (now famous for his award-winning plays *The Evacuees* and *Bar Mitzvah Boy*) concentrated on the lighter side of *Coronation Street*'s characters and brought a great deal of humour to the programme; John Finch, more solemn as befits the later author of *Family at War* and *Sam*, brought a more serious element, and Peter Eckersley, a student of Lancashire life, injected a contemporary realism and a true nostalgia, both perfectly suited to the programme.

After the writers came the directors. Although producers came from a variety of backgrounds there is little doubt that those with directorial experience were most suited to the job. They were well versed in the intricacies of scheduling, they had worked at close quarters with the cast, they knew what was wanted from a script even if they themselves were not equipped to shape the finished article. Which was why I, as executive producer, also took on the role of script editor when needed. This little band of director/producers, all members of the *Coronation Street* family in that they had at some time directed the programme, included Michael Cox, Howard Baker, June Howson and Richard Everitt, who during my later absence producing *City '68* took over the reins of executive producer. Following them came Susi Hush, Brian Armstrong (now head of Granada's comedy department), Eric (Taffy) Prytherch, who was later to direct and produce two comedy series I had created, *The Life of Riley* and *Leave It to Charlie* and, lastly, Bill Podmore who has held the office longer than anyone except myself and looks like beating me out of sight. Bill's paradoxical mixture of an easy-going personality and a stubborn obstinacy to get his own way made him a natural for the job. An ex-comedy producer himself, he has carried on the comedy tradition of the programme without abandoning its more serious side. The years since 1973 when I gave up my staff job at Granada and became once again a freelance writer, have been, first under Eric Prytherch and later under Bill Podmore, very happy years indeed.

It is little short of amazing, looking back at the abundance of names in this chapter, that the programme's life has not been subjected to violent change. I have never been one of those who believed that a programme can exert its own authority. Programmes are run by people and it is the people who decide what shall and shall not be done. However, *Coronation Street* did have its own peculiarities. Everyone concerned, writers, actors and technicians, were committed to conserving what was best in the programme and resisting what they considered would be bad. It was this which probably stood in the way of the changes which might have been imposed by any new producer. A slight frown from Violet Carson or Pat Phoenix when the new boy made some careless suggestion, a cry of 'You can't do that!' from a horrified technician at the hint of some new-fangled electronic gimmickry or the sudden silence at a story conference when a plot was mooted which didn't fit, all helped to deter the would-be radical. And if that wasn't enough there was always the underlying fear that, not knowing the magic ingredient which had served *Coronation Street* so well over the years, it was always possible, by the accident of change, to remove that ingredient forever.

There were, of course, more subtle differences between reigns. Not least when king was succeeded by queen. The ladies tended to introduce a more romantic vein into our

67

stories and this was no bad thing in itself when one considers that women had always formed the bulk of the *Coronation Street* audience. Women too tend to be feminist at times and it was Susi Hush who thumbed her nose at her male associates and took most of the lady members of the cast plus a lady writer and herself on a filming jaunt to Majorca. Only the director, probably by some accident of scheduling, was a man.

If there were differences between producers on some issues, there was total uniformity on others. It has already been described how the serial stuck grimly to its row of terraced houses at a time when, throughout the country, these were being replaced by high-rise flats, and has lived to see the process reversed. Nor were the programme's producers merely concerned with the preservation of architectural values. *Coronation Street* has lived through the swinging sixties and the savage seventies without taking advantage – if that is the phrase – of the general lowering of moral attitudes and the advent of almost total artistic permissiveness. Quite apart from my belief – which is shared by many of my friends in the industry – that the frontiers of good taste have been pushed back much too far, there are sound commercial reasons for *Coronation Street*'s seemingly reactionary stance. On the subject of language the programme has never gone in for four-letter words although every writer and producer is well aware of the fact that the Len Fairdoughs of this world are not averse to using a few when the occasion arises. But those same Len Fairdoughs demand a higher standard from television than they do from themselves and their own workmates. They are conscious of the fact that they are watching television with their wives, their mothers and their children and whilst there will always be a proportion who will 'cuss and blind' in front of anyone the vast majority prefer to shield their women-folk and children from this kind of language.

Mere antipathy to bad language is not the only, nor even

the chief reason for keeping it out of *Coronation Street*. The programme has always been transmitted in the early evening and we have always sought a family audience. Large numbers of young people watch the programme and they are joined twice a week by a major proportion of the country's senior citizens. It is this element which swells *Coronation Street*'s audience and lifts the programme's viewing figures firmly into the top half of the Top Ten and, as an entertainer, it would be highly unprofessional of any producer to ignore them. These are the people who are most easily offended and until it can be argued that bad language in some way enriches their experience there is little point in shocking them. There is however another, more selfish, reason for our apparent puritanism. Constant use of 'hard' language tends to devalue the commodity. Used often enough any word or phrase will lose its strength and the time will soon come – indeed it could be said that it has already come – when the most extreme swearing will have totally lost its impact. It then falls to the writer to coin new words which will, when required, have the desired shock effect. *Coronation Street* resisted the use of the word 'bloody' until episode 190 when Len Fairclough, suffering under the stress of the kidnapping of his friend's baby, used the word to Emily Nugent and immediately apologized. Those days have gone forever. Today swearing, particularly in television comedy, is often used as a crutch by the writer devoid of true comic ideas. Spurred on by the fact that it invariably raises a laugh from the studio audience such a writer forgets that among such audiences it is only embarrassing to be out of step. If one laughs everybody laughs but in the sitting-room there are other embarrassments. Unhappily this isn't universally appreciated. I have known scriptwriters who wouldn't dream of telling a particular dirty joke if a strange lady – or at times even a strange man – were in the company, yet who would happily include the same joke in a script which went out to a totally unknown audience of twenty million people.

There are times when I wonder if *Coronation Street* isn't being unduly cautious but I console myself with the thought that what you've never had you never miss. In all my years as producer of the serial I never received a single letter from a viewer complaining that there was not enough bad language in our programme.

CHAPTER SEVEN

'Ee, I could write a book!'

Elsie Tanner

Not only Elsie could write a book. We all could. Everyone on God's earth has a story to tell, be it bitter, comic, pain-filled or idyllic.

There is a great deal of resentment felt by those who feel they could write professionally but are denied the chance for those who have been lucky enough to break through and earn their living at this most rewarding of professions. The resentment is understandable. Most of my readers will at some time have heard someone criticizing some television programme or another by saying 'I could have done better myself.' Indeed my readers may well have said it themselves and to a certain degree they could have been right. However, it is not quite as easy as it may sound. A scriptwriter's job demands a certain kind of talent, hard though that talent may be to define. He must have the ability to hear what he is giving his characters to say before he puts it on the page, to interweave plot and inconsequentiality in the right proportions, to raise his dialogue those important two degrees into the bizarre so that it is both exciting and interesting to the listener and yet sounds like everyday talk. In addition to talent, and possibly more important, he needs self-confidence. Told to write an episode about an air crash in the mountains of Patagonia, he must be able to describe both the events and the terrain without either having been in an air crash or that part of the world. The professional writer will use his imagination with confidence and, amazingly, will never be far from the truth.

With the benefit of total recall (the ability to remember conversations held at the age of three), the writer need never worry about a source of material, as his own life will supply everything that is necessary. John Finch and Jack Rosenthal both enjoy this gift. Dramatizations of their own lives have been woven into series and plays to the vast enjoyment of a wide audience. I am not so lucky. When I look back my memory fades somewhere in my teens but this is not to say that I have ignored my own life during my career as a writer. In *Coronation Street* I gave Frank Barlow (Ken's father played by the late Frank Pemberton) my own army background in the 7th Cheshires. This way I knew that whenever he talked about his war-time days he was describing the genuine article. In later years I bequeathed my never-forgotten army number 4129818 and my early experience in the forces to Philip Ashton, the eldest son in *Family at War*.

Apart from the odd snippets of character and conversation culled from the reality of my own memory, my life provided other opportunities for dramatic reconstruction. One arose from a string of disturbing events which took place over the mid to late 1960s. It first came to my notice in 1965 that I was being impersonated. Not criminally but sufficiently often and in such circumstances that it proved worrisome. I was producing the programme at the time and it was a telephone call to the *Coronation Street* office by a Manchester publican which started the ball rolling. The previous evening a man had walked into his bar and, after a couple of drinks, had introduced himself as the *Coronation Street* producer. The pub's regulars had gathered round him, he had unfailingly stood his corner when required and a jolly evening had been enjoyed by all. This in itself was strange. I had always believed that a cloak of anonymity, particularly in public houses, was the best defence against being hustled into a corner and bombarded with criticism. It appeared that Mr X knew how to pick his watering places. What was even stranger was the action of the landlord. It was only at the end of the evening in question that a couple of unguarded remarks caused mine host to doubt his client's authenticity. When he rang me the following morning he became the first and last 'victim' to be sufficiently unsure to check with the source. A possible reason for this is that our mystery man improved with practice!

A check was made on another occasion but by a third party rather than the dupe herself. One Monday morning I received a telephone call from a tremulous young female voice informing me that the owner's widowed mother had rung her over the weekend in a high state of excitement. The mother was the licensee of a Liverpool public house and on the previous Friday night a man had walked into her establishment and, after two hours solitary drinking, had quietly introduced himself to her as Harry Kershaw, *Coronation Street*'s producer. He told an amazingly credible story. According to him, Arthur Leslie who played Jack Walker, landlord of the Rovers Return, had expressed a wish to leave the programme and because his character was so closely linked with that of his wife, played by Doris Speed, it was decided that both must leave the programme. The production team had decided after great debate that the search for a replacement should not be left to the Casting Department. Criticism had been received from the general public – and particularly from people in the licensed trade – that 'Jack' and 'Annie' were not particularly adept in pulling pints. This was absolutely true although probably due more to lack of technical facilities than dexterity.

The impostor, who obviously had some inside knowledge of the workings of the programme, had gone on to say that a further decision had been taken. It had been decided, he said, that instead of casting actors to take over in the Rovers Return and then hoping for the best, we would solve our problem the other way around – we would cast from the ranks of the licensed trade and train our choices to be actors or actresses. For this reason he was visiting various pubs in the North-West in an attempt to find likely candidates, and he told the delighted landlady that she was very high on his short list. He had been watching her and had been very impressed by her manner. When, on the telephone, I asked the daughter what had been the upshot she told me that on the Saturday morning when he left he had promised that he would be getting in touch with her and arranging camera tests at Granada's studios in Manchester. As he had arrived on the Friday evening and didn't leave until Saturday it was fairly obvious that he had enjoyed hospitality beyond the usual pint of bitter beer and it was this that caused me, after explaining the situation to the distraught daughter, to call in the police. They came with alacrity but no great hope of success. Obviously one couldn't keep a police patrol in every public house in case someone should walk in proclaiming that he was me. However they were sympathetic, said they'd do what they could, and asked me if I'd notify them of any further developments.

The story has an interesting conclusion. A couple of weeks after the police first visited me I received a telephone call from a gentleman who introduced himself as 'Norman'. 'You remember me,' he said, 'we had a drink last night in that pub on Hyde Road with my pal George.' Of course I hadn't and I told him so and I also gave him chapter and verse on the impostor who, it appears, had been very knowledgeable about Granada, had stood his corner as before and had promised that if ever Norman and George wanted a guided tour of Granada all they had to do was telephone. I could only apologize and asked for their assistance.

'It would help me,' I said, 'if you could take this story to your local police.'

There was a long pause, then: 'We *are* the local police,' said Norman.

In all, I learned of a dozen or so deceptions but the ones I knew of were not the ones that most bothered me. In these cases I could tell the victims the truth and, disturbing for them though it may have been (it was no joke, for instance, to have one's entire complement of hotel bedrooms booked by a fictional producer!), at least there was no lasting ill-will towards Granada or myself. But what of those victims who never learned the truth? What of the lady victuallers who are still waiting to embark on a star-studded career and are either too shy or too embarrassed to pursue the matter? I can only hope they read this book.

The problem was eventually solved by a simple expedient. The story of the impersonations, together with my photograph, was printed in the *Morning Advertiser*, the licensed trade's paper. Somehow our impostor must have realized the danger – he never appeared again.

When in the late 1960s I was asked if I would like to contribute to Granada's *Crown Court* this story immediately sprang to mind. The fictional version however bore one essential difference from the original. The poseur had been caught and brought to trial for impersonation, something that reality has not yet achieved.

This opportunity to lay the events of one's own life and the dubious benefits of one's opinions before a multi-million audience is only one of the joys of writing for television. An abiding interest in one's fellow man is an essential ingredient in the make-up of any writer of contemporary drama and here again there is an opportunity – indeed a necessity – to examine one's friends, relatives and acquaintances in the hope that they will throw up something of dramatic value. Naturally the examination takes place from a safe distance and although 'Don't say anything in front of Harry or you will find yourself in *Coronation Street*' is something I often hear, I have yet to meet any 'victim' who recognized himself on the screen. There are, of course, always the unhappy cranks. Like the lady many years ago who wrote threatening to call in the police as it was patently obvious that someone from our programme was listening at her key-hole, so many of her intimate details had been revealed. Had her allegations been true she would have been an exception.

Most of my acquaintances who have been 'dramatized' not only failed to recognize themselves but refused to believe that anyone on earth could possibly behave in such a manner. A case springs to mind. Many years ago I used to frequent a Cheshire pub where the landlord, a jovial man, had old-fashioned ideas about his function. He believed deeply in the 'Mine Host' syndrome and considered it his job to mingle with his friends on the public side of the bar and never to involve himself with the more menial tasks of serving drinks and the like. I decided after a few weeks observation to introduce him into *Coronation Street*. I started a story where Jack Walker of the Rovers Return decided that he too was going to become Mine Host. His wife Annie didn't take too kindly to the idea but decided to indulge him and I wrote a sequence where Jack moved from behind the bar and began to socialize with his customers.

Some weeks later I watched the episode when it was transmitted and later that same evening strolled down to my local for a pint with my friends. At nine o'clock, the jovial landlord came downstairs after his nightly ration of television, threw a cheerful wave to his perspiring staff and proceeded to mix with his customers. He spotted me. 'Watched your show tonight,' he said accusingly. 'And I'm blowed if I know where you pick these things up! That bit where the landlord decided he wasn't going to do any work. All he was going to do was chat with his customers!' He laughed sympathetically. 'Eh, lad you've got a lot to learn! He wouldn't last five minutes at that game'! What could I do but apologize for my ignorance?

Many times as *Coronation Street*'s producer and less often as one of its writers, it has been suggested to me that I could, if I tried, bring down the Government. There may indeed be a germ of truth in this. When one hears that a children's programme has collected, in no time at all, millions of pounds for the refugees of South-East Asia or that some magazine programme has appealed for and received countless thousands of toys and necessities for distribution to the deprived young and the needy old at Christmas one begins to realize the power of television. Indeed many an envious political, commercial and charitable eye has been cast in our direction, and with this power in mind every television writer has to battle against not only the persuasions of others but with his own. Political persuasions probably offer the easiest example. It would be asking too much of a mature writer of contemporary drama never to expect him to colour his scripts with his own beliefs. 'Colouring', however, is one thing, 'daubing' is another and on those rare occasions when, due to an excess of zeal, a writer is unable to differentiate between the two and to impose the right amount of self-censorship on his work it falls to someone else to put matters right.

Censorship is an emotive word but mainly, it appears, when shouted to the masses. Whilst I have known a great deal of heat to be generated by the subject at writers' meetings, I have met and talked to few individual writers who were bothered by the phenomenon. Most of them are sensible enough to censor their own work and to follow commonsense rules without having those rules imposed upon them by others. Naturally there are exceptions. The more intense a writer's feelings, the more likely he is to indulge himself in those 'excesses of zeal'. Jim Allen, undoubtedly one of Britain's best political dramatists, started his writing career on *Coronation Street* as a result of the most persuasive letter I have ever received from an agent. Harvey Unna, who represented Jim, wrote to me whilst I was producing *Coronation Street*, asking me to see his protégé. His description of Jim and his abilities was so compelling that I had no option but to see his client as soon as I could. This resulted in Jim taking a short writer's course at Granada and then joining the *Coronation Street* writing team. His stay with us was fruitful – to both sides I hope – but short.

Although I have always believed that there is a place for political drama I have never subscribed to the principle

77

that the theatre and the television studios are one huge soap-box for the use of political oratory. It would be tempting to report that Jim Allen and I fought bitter battles over this expurgation of his work but happily this didn't happen. Jim, a sensible man, realized that the climate of *Coronation Street* did not allow for any kind of strong political statement and eventually he left us for a more permissive atmosphere where, there is no doubt whatsoever, he has done extremely well.

Coronation Street's writing teams have always offered a cross-section of political opinion. Injected sparingly these opinions lend a reality to the programme which is missing in those serials which deliberately avoid any mention of politics. A fair balance is maintained not by having Len Fairclough spout Socialist dogma in one episode and Conservative doctrine in the next (which would make a travesty of his character) but by evolving over the years characters of varying political persuasions. Ken Barlow, for instance, has always been left-wing whilst Annie Walker has always leant – sometimes to the point of falling over – to the right. This system of politicizing our various characters means that if any writer has a social comment to make he is in a position to choose his own mouthpiece knowing that he will not be guilty of character assassination.

General rather than specific comment on political lines is rather harder to achieve. During the run up to the 1964 General Election it was decided that we could not, in all conscience, ignore the event. How to do it without causing offence? Knowing how difficult it is to please everybody the only alternative is to displease everybody and this we did. Ena Sharples was visited by canvassers of the three main parties and was seen, at different times, to make appointments with them to come back to chat to her at eight o'clock that evening. At eight o'clock, inside Ena's vestry, the astonished canvassers were introduced to each other by a Machiavellian Ena who bestowed upon them the famous look and said, 'Now I know you all want to do something for me so let's be hearing what it is. Who's first?' At which point we faded the scene to avoid embarrassment.

It would be difficult to leave the subject of politics in drama without touching on a strange phenomenon. Whilst there are numerous left-wing writers putting their beliefs into the mouths of actors, the same can in no way be said for the adherents of the Right. Merely from their offerings on the TV screen I could name a dozen patently Socialist writers but, taking the same yardstick, I could only guess at a couple who might possibly be ardent Tories. Why is this? Because, where propaganda is concerned, the Socialists believe that nowhere is sacrosanct whereas Tories hold that there is only one political theatre and that the Palace at Westminster? Possible, but I doubt it. Could it be part of a deep-dyed plot by International Socialism to infiltrate the stages and the studios of the Western democracies? I doubt that too. A much more plausible explanation is that Socialism, playing as it does on the emotions and leaning heavily on nostalgia, provides much more interesting material than the matter-of fact policies of Conservatism. It would be difficult indeed to fashion a rousing Play of the Week out of Keith Joseph and his monetarist policy but give a committed writer Workers' Control and Wedgwood Benn and he'll make your flesh creep. I can't see a series in the CBI but the National Coal Board and the NUM could keep three television channels happily supplied with drama for years. In fact, they *have* done. When *Sam*, *The Stars Look Down*, *When the Boat Comes In* and *Days of Hope* were on the small screen it was difficult to meet an actor whose face wasn't streaked with coal dust. The Devil may have the best tunes but there's little doubt that the Left has the best scripts!

If I keep repeating that writing for *Coronation Street* is a joy, it can only be because it is. I find it difficult to express the pleasure I feel sitting at my typewriter and savouring the task of writing a Rovers Return scene for Annie, Bet, Betty, Len, Elsie or indeed any combination or permutation of the regular cast. These are not shadowy undrawn figures as they would be were I writing some speculative play as yet uncast – these are people with a long life of their own. I found this ready-made quality a great advantage when I was asked to write the three *Coronation Street* novels.

I was able to close my eyes and see my characters in the wider world which the novel can reach. Studio space is badly restricted and each pair of episodes must be played out in five tiny sets, but in the novel the writer is offered not only the world but all of space in which to operate and it was an added pleasure to be able to take my old friends farther afield. Not too far of course to be unreal. To North Wales on a competition-won holiday, every inch of the way there and back to Blackpool on a day out, on bus rides, on visits to the Town Hall, and a hundred other activities which had been denied to us by the confines of television and the restrictions of time.

The writing of novels is only one of the ancillary activities open to the *Coronation Street* writer. I have written countless articles and short stories based on the programme and its characters but the strangest demand made on me as a writer fell outside the world of prose. And whilst I was producing rather than writing.

At the beginning of my stint as producer I had agreed with the management that I should 'keep my hand in' by writing three or four episodes each year. As my office at Granada resembled Piccadilly Circus at rush hour and concentration on a script was impossible, the actual writing took place at home but there was so much pleasure in returning to my old love after months of desk-bound administration that the extra hours didn't bother me at all.

One of the episodes I wrote during this period (episode 1244 for the statistically minded) was due to be transmitted just before Christmas 1972 and had as one of its themes the growing relationship between Ken Barlow, at that time a widower, and Norma Ford (played by Diana Davies), the current assistant at the corner shop. Ken was privately tutoring Norma in English literature and, helped by the heady atmosphere of romantic poetry, the impressionable girl rapidly fell in love with her teacher. Unfortunately it wasn't reciprocated but she didn't realize this and her hopes were raised sky high when Ken introduced a particular piece of verse into their studies. At first sight this was a declaration of love on his part but there was a sting in the tail of the poem which, due to a timely interruption (and the dramatic needs of the long-running serial) wasn't to destroy Norma's ecstasy until the next episode. What we were looking for then was a romantic poem with a sting in the tail and I set the storyline writers the job of finding one.

The rest of the script had been written and all that was needed was the injection of the appropriate lines, but three weeks later, despite an exhaustive search, they still hadn't been found. By this time the director was clamouring for his finished script and there was only one thing to do – write the poem myself. As both writer and producer the responsibility was mine so, telling my secretary to keep my door closed and the telephones silent, I sat at my desk with a blank sheet of paper in front of me and waited desperately for inspiration. If necessity really is the mother of invention this was the time to put it to the test. Half an hour later the following had emerged . . .

> To talk with you.
> To walk, your hand in mine,
> through well-remembered woods
> and watch the sunlight searching
> through the trees
> to find your eyes.
> Such are the pleasures of my life.
> To be with you.
> To feel your thoughts, unspoken,

meet with mine
and lead our lips and eager hands
to mutual delights.
These are my pleasures too.

It was here that the interruption came. And then the sting . . .

But doubts arise
to mist those woods and cloud those eyes.
For, without love,
all passions die
and soon the last remaining pleasure is goodbye.

The response was amazing. No sooner had the episode been seen on the screen than letters started flooding in. Could I have a copy of the poem? Who wrote it? One imaginative gentleman said that of course it was written by Shelley but where could he find it? He'd searched and searched . . .

We decided, in order not to disappoint our viewers too much, to tell any enquirer that the lines had been written by John Graham, an obscure Scottish poet who had lived in Edinburgh at the turn of the eighteenth century and who had died, tragically, at the age of twenty-three.

It could be argued that to provide a writer with ready-made characters is to take away from him part of the joy of creation but I have never found this a drawback in *Coronation Street*. On the one hand there are always new characters joining us who need to be 'filled out' and, on the other, the characters who have been with us for many years are still only half explored. Each writer not only has his own favourite characters (though he would never admit to them), he also has his favourite moods. The Ogdens, Hilda and Stan, arguably one of the funniest cross-talk teams on television, are to my mind at their best when they are poignant. Hilda, thin and defiant, defending the fat, lazy Stan against an unkind world; Annie Walker, against all odds, introducing gracious living into a backstreet pub; Ena, cold-eyed, railing against bureaucracy; and Elsie Tanner laughing in the face of a world which has battered her for years and hasn't stopped yet – are all pearls beyond price to any writer.

Just as different producers stamped, though not indelibly, their impressions on the *Street* so each writer brought his or her individualism to the writing of the programme. The most obvious division is by sex. Whilst all the writing team, men and women, believe that each of us can write equally well for every character, there is little doubt that the woman's angle is best left to the women writers. Adele Rose, the show's second longest serving writer, is currently the only woman on the team but sterling service during recent years was given by Kay McManus, Paula Milne and Susan Pleat.

It is *Coronation Street*'s great good fortune and a measure of its attractiveness that over the twenty years of its life it has been supported by only three writing teams. As any football manager will tell you the successful squad contains a judicious blend of youthful enthusiasm and mature experience and it is this mixture which has kept the show going over the years. The first team, put together hurriedly but happily in the later months of 1960, had for its backbone Tony Warren, Adele Rose, Jack Rosenthal, John Finch, Peter Eckersley and myself. Our middle period – the late sixties and early seventies – saw the departure of Jack Rosenthal and John Finch for pastures new and the team formed itself around Peter Eckersley, Adele Rose, Geoffrey Lancashire, Jim Allen, Leslie Duxbury, Brian Finch and Susan Pleat. Currently the first-choice writers are Leslie Duxbury, Julian Roach, John Stevenson, Adele Rose, Barry Hill and myself.

All these teams have, over the years, been supported by a pool of talented reserves. Currently that support comes from Tony Perrin and Peter Whalley. Theirs is a more difficult job than that of the regular writer. They do not have the advantage of constant involvement in the programme but, although they may be called upon to write only one episode each three months, the continuity and characterization in that episode must be as strong as in any other.

Continuity is always of vital importance. Every third Monday the producer meets with his writers, his story-line writers and the casting director to plan the stories for a further six episodes. Plans are laid some ten weeks in advance which is to say that a story conference held at the beginning of January would be discussing episodes which would be seen on the screen from mid March to early April. The fact that our thoughts are so far in the future in no way cools down the proceedings. Story conferences are gruelling affairs which can go on unbroken, except for an even more argumentative lunch break, for eight or nine hours. Everyone has his own idea how a particular story should be played out, where the emphasis should lie and which characters would be best employed, and feelings often run high. Not that this bothers us. The day the story conference leans back in its collective chair, yawns and rubber-stamps every suggestion without dissent is the day they start to chip out *Coronation Street*'s headstone.

At the end of each tumultuous conference the programme secretary is left with a welter of argument and counter-argument scattered over the pages of her shorthand notebook. Either Carole or Diane, the current secretaries, will then translate the unspeakable into standard English and publish the result. The top copy goes to the two story-line writers, currently Esther Rose and Peter Tonkinson, who have themselves taken copious notes at the meeting. It is their job to prepare the breakdowns of six episodes from the mass of story material agreed at the conference. Each breakdown will tell the relevant stories scene by scene and will indicate to the writer which characters are to be involved and where the scene is to take place. Naturally there are restrictions on the number of sets which can be used and as a general rule we use no more than five interior sets each week plus, if facilities are available, a scene or two in each episode shot on location either on mobile videotape or on film.

The job of the storyline writer is much more complicated than it may at first appear. Each contract artist is guaranteed a number of episodes over each period and it is up to the storyline writers to ensure that these guarantees are met. As there are rarely fewer than twenty-two contract artists at any one time it can be seen that this is no simple task. Moreover – and most importantly – the storyline writers have the initial responsibility for the smooth flow of story from one episode to the next. Continuity is without doubt the most difficult part of a serial's life. Not only does it demand that the plot should progress logically from week to week but it must take account of the relationships between characters, and with a cast of over twenty the combinations and permutations of those relationships are considerable. We cannot for instance have Elsie Tanner smiling warmly at Annie Walker the episode after she has had a blazing row with her across the bar of the Rovers Return. Even though that story may have finished, the strained atmosphere must continue.

Perhaps the most troublesome area of continuity, because mistakes in that area are most easily spotted by the viewers, covers the personal data of our running characters. Ena Sharples celebrates her birthday on 14 November and given an average audience of sixteen million viewers per episode a few seconds on a pocket calculator will show that that birthday is shared by 44,000 of those viewers. Heaven help us then if we change her birthdate! Theoretically 44,000 letters will reach us telling us we have made a mistake. Not only do viewers remember anniversaries, they even store away those likes and dislikes they share with their favourite stars. In the first episode Ena Sharples was heard to say that she didn't like chocolate éclairs and when some eight years later we were careless enough to see her not only eating one but asking for another, we received a howl of disapproval from those viewers who shared Ena's dislike of that pastry.

In spite of the perils and pitfalls which lie at every turn, however, *Coronation Street* maintains a fairly good record. From Eric Rosser, the programme's archivist, through the storyline writers, the scriptwriters, the producer's office, the artists, directors and floor crew, a host of sharp eyes are kept open for any semblance of a mistake. And still we make them!

The most important facet of continuity however is not of fact but of style. Not only must the characters, episode by episode, continue to behave and to talk in the same way, but the whole atmosphere of the *Street* and its surroundings must remain unchanged. It is to the eternal credit of all the writers involved on the programme since its inception that this style has been maintained. There are those viewers who profess to be able to pick out an individual writer from the first few minutes of his or her episode but I have to confess that, after a near-lifetime on the show, I cannot do so. Nor do I, as do some, see *Coronation Street* writers as mere copyists, and the varied expertise shown by Jack Rosenthal in his plays, John Finch in his family sagas and Geoffrey Lancashire in his comedies tends to prove me right. In fact the minimal variations in style from one episode to the next underline rather than decry the talent of successive scriptwriting teams.

The varied talents of the original writing team led, at the beginning of 1963, to the formation of the writers' consortium Group North. Television, I had always felt, wasted ability to an alarming extent. Most television executives and producers believed (and still do, for that matter) that if a writer could not start with a blank sheet of paper and, from the riches of his own mind, create a finished, produceable script, he was not worthy of his title. It was not sufficient to be able to weave marvellous stories or create intriguing characters or write matchless dialogue – if all three talents were not contained within the one individual, that individual was, regretfully, shown the door. I had recurring

mental visions of two writers, rejected by separate producers on grounds of inadequacy, one a poor hand at
dialogue, but a spellbinding storyteller and the other a
plotless wordsmith of Wildean proportions, meeting in
Granada's foyer. On the way out. And parting again, never
to know what might have been.

Tony Warren was a case in point. In submitting the
first five episodes of *Coronation Street* he had made Granada
an offer they couldn't refuse but he was by no means what
the company considered to be the complete writer. They
were partly right. Although one of the best creators of
character in the business, he lacked the stamina to turn out
the endless stream of dialogue which television demanded.
And because of this he languished where he should have
prospered. Had he been put to work creating characters
for other writers to develop he would have made a considerable contribution to television drama. But current
thinking, coupled with his understandable desire, shared by
most of his fellow writers, to do everything himself, denied
TV drama a stream of characters as valuable to the
medium as were Dickens's creations to the literature of the
nineteenth century.

It was this feeling of frustration with the system which
led me, in 1963, to put forward the idea of a writers' group.
The success we had enjoyed with a closely-knit writing
team in *Coronation Street* was to be continued in *The Villains*, an
hour-length series I began to produce in late 1963 on one of
my 'release' periods from the *Street*. I had always believed
that by keeping a close collaboration with my writers from
the earliest stage (*before* an idea had even germinated) we
arrived much more happily at a finished script. Give a writer
carte blanche, say to him 'This is roughly what our show is about.
Go away and write us a script' and he is likely (a) to disappoint in style and content and (b) to make demands of setting
and cast which the programme cannot meet. Moreover, if the
same casual instructions are given to a number of writers, two
or more may come up with the same story. Many a script has

been consigned to the wastepaper basket and a fee wasted by a producer failing to tell each of his writers what the others were doing. But, I reasoned, if the producer talked over each script from the idea stage, there was unlikely to be duplication. We took this thought even further. Many story ideas for *The Villains* sprang from the production team and were offered to individual writers to develop. I never knew a professional writer refuse this 'service'. They would invariably make alterations and stamp their individuality on the script but they were happy in the knowledge that the story itself fitted the programme brief and it was unlikely to be rejected by the producer who had thought it up in the first place! It was these obvious benefits of teamwork which led me to my conclusion. If we could work happily together under the auspices of one programme why not use our co-operative feelings to *create* programmes?

Group North was launched on 25 April 1963 as a limited company with an issued share capital of £1,000 and seven directors – Cyril Abraham, Harry Driver, Peter Eckersley, John Finch, myself, Vince Powell and Jack Rosenthal. We were later joined by George Reed, an ex-schoolmaster from East Anglia who entered our world by acting as secretary to Harry Driver and who was the first to leave us and go back to his old love, teaching.

Our first few meetings were totally businesslike and highly unproductive and we soon exchanged our formal suite of offices in the city for the back room of the Pineapple, a pub behind Granada's studios. There, on alternate Friday evenings, we drank and discussed our communal and individual needs. Writing is a lonely occupation and a few sociable hours in the company of one's fellows helped dispel the feeling of isolation. We discovered a universal fear: beset by a workless six months, we would, being self-employed, find ourselves ignored by an otherwise benevolent State and forced to live on whatever savings we may have put by. It was this prospect which led us to form a fund from

88

our incomes against such a possibility. Happily it was used only once but it was there if needed. Not that all our needs were economic. We used each other as sounding-boards. A writer may dream up a series idea in the solitude of his own den but he will not believe it to be either good or bad until someone else says so. So we tried our ideas on each other and pronounced on them. And then, some months after our formation, we came up with our first successful group conception.

It all started as something of a joke at one of our fortnightly meetings. We had started the proceedings with a light-hearted declaration that we wouldn't move from the place before we came up with a series idea. Inside an hour, a concept had emerged concerning two itinerant, non-Union workers who travelled the country searching for tough, well-paid work. A sort of English Western, we told ourselves, with our heroes, at the start of each episode, standing on the brow of the hill gazing at the town below before they strolled down and involved themselves dramatically in the lives of the inhabitants. George Reed gave us the title. In East Anglia, he told us, the nomadic worker was known as a catch hand. And 'Catch Hand' it was. We discussed a batch of storylines and I was deputed to type up the format and send it to our agent, Kenneth Ewing of Fraser and Dunlop. From then on events moved at a brisk pace. In the space of a few months the BBC had bought the idea, scripts had been commissioned and written and the show put into production. On Wednesday, 1 July 1964 the first episode of *Catch Hand*, bearing the magical credit 'Series created by Group North' went on the air.

We weren't happy with the production but then few writers ever are and, in any event, that's another story. What was unusual about the show was that it was not only the first group concept but the last. And for the very best of reasons. When Group North was first mooted, everyone concerned, with the sole exception of the late Cyril Abraham, was connected with *Coronation Street*. As Derek Jewell said in his article on the group in the *Sunday Times* Colour Magazine of 28 June, 1964, '*Coronation Street*, which in twenty years may be seen as a kind of memorial to the writers of Group North, was in fact the springboard for the organization.'

He went on to quote me. ' "When we got to know each other," says Kershaw, "it seemed silly all sitting around in our own backyards beating our brains out. Committee work in the best sense was already beginning to work on the *Street*. I didn't see why we couldn't produce good ideas for every kind of series by working together." ' Which is, partially, what happened. We produced the ideas, not collectively, but individually. A sympathetic explosion of luck, persistence and a desire for work showered commissions and jobs on all but one of us. John Finch took the road which was to lead to his successful series of sagas beginning with *Family at War*; Jack Rosenthal developed a taste for comedy and playwriting (and producers developed a taste for *him*) which launched *The Dustbinmen*, *The Lovers*, and a host of marvellously entertaining plays; Peter Eckersley, after a flurry as a playwright, began to produce and eventually became Granada's Head of Drama; Harry Driver and Vince Powell were seduced to London to act as comedy advisers to Thames Television whilst I took a staff appointment with Granada and returned full time to the *Street* as producer and later executive producer. Only Cyril Abraham failed to take off. During the last few months of Group North's brief life we had tried, unsuccessfully, to place an idea of Cyril's based on the adventures of the crew of a coaster plying British waters. But he wasn't to be denied. He took his idea back in time, widened his canvas in more ways than one and created *The Onedin Line*.

The formation of Group North had caused something of a flutter in television's executive dovecotes. Coming as it did at a time when union muscles were beginning to flex within the industry, any co-operative of this kind was bound to be viewed with suspicion. What were we up to? Did we aim to achieve a stranglehold on certain series – particularly *Coronation Street*? It was my task to allay these fears and this I was able to do with total sincerity. Nothing had been farther from our thoughts. Whilst most writers I knew would happily follow each other into the nearest bar we were, as a profession, not terribly good with banners and even worse at anything as disciplined as marching.

The diversification practised by the writer-members of Group North has been carried on by subsequent writers for *Coronation Street*. Not only did the show give most of them their first television credit, it demanded that they try their hand at every aspect of their craft. It is not surprising that *Street* writers have since written satire, contemporary drama and comedy in all its varied forms. Writers who started their professional careers on the *Street* have since contributed, in the drama field, to *The Odd Man, The Villains, Z Cars, Crown Court, Village Hall, Sam, Shabby Tiger, Armchair Theatre, Play of the Week, Play of the Month, Fallen Hero, All Creatures Great and Small, This Year, Next Year* amongst a host of others, and in comedy to *Nearest and Dearest, The Dustbinmen, The Lovers, Bless This House, Cuckoo Waltz, Life of Riley, Leave It to Charlie, Mind Your Language, Selwyn Froggitt, Love Thy Neighbour, Robin's Nest* and many more. Some have left to concentrate on their chosen field, others have stayed. For myself, I never want to leave. There are times when I deliver my script into the hands of the producer and wish the programme had more time, more space, more money to lavish upon it. And then I count my blessings. I have mixed writing and producing for *Coronation Street* for its first ten years. Since then I have been a regular contributor of scripts. It has given me a good living, an entrée into what is still an exciting world, an opportunity to place my work before Britain's largest audience and the chance to work as part of what I consider to be the best team in television. I hope they'll have me as long as I can hit a typewriter key.

CHAPTER EIGHT

'Acting? It's a bobby's job!'

Betty Turpin

Did Betty Turpin, the cheerful barmaid of the Rovers Return, really believe, as do so many people, that the life of the actor is a sinecure, a cushy number that pays highly for little work, or was she, through her special knowledge, employing a little irony? Having been married to a 'bobby' for many years she knew better than most that the policeman's lot brought long, unsocial hours, relatively little pay and a life spent in full view of a public who often expected more than it was humanly possible to give. Add to those positive disadvantages the undisputed fact that the odds against being employed at any particular moment are twenty to one and you have the life of the actor. Not that they look at it like that. Most actors (and I use the word bisexually) appear to enjoy their insecure existence. Once having caught the bug they follow their chosen path to the often bitter end. But despite the heartaches, the broken marriages, the running battles with the tax man and the constant changes in public preference, the actor remains the most convivial of companions. Happiest amongst his own kind (and aren't we all?) he can nevertheless walk into any company and remain polite, well informed, witty and entertaining. It is no coincidence that the most successful of the *This Is Your Life* half hours have been devoted to entertainers. They have no illusions about being illusions. They know very well, television actors in particular, that they are a nationalized commodity and have long passed into public ownership. And no property is more public than the people of *Coronation Street*.

92

Through no fault of its own, the serial appears to be at the centre of that area of confusion between actor and character, fact and fiction. The long life of its characters and their close resemblance to many in its wide audience have built up an affection vastly different from the mere feeling of respect shown by an earlier public for its idols of stage and cinema screen. No one in the fifties would, for instance, on seeing Alec Guinness walking from the Opera House to Manchester's Midland Hotel, have dreamt of shouting 'Hello, Alec!' across the road. Nowadays, however, vast numbers of viewers feel themselves to be on Christian name terms, not with the actors and actresses concerned, but with the characters they portray. And not only to exchange greetings with them but to share their problems and at times to seek their help. I remember meeting Frank Pemberton in Granada's foyer one morning in *Coronation Street*'s first year of life.

'I could have done with you a few minutes ago,' he said. 'You could have written a few lines of script for me.' He went on to explain. He was playing Frank Barlow, head of the strife-torn Barlow family who lived at number three, and their current disagreement was over elder son Ken's involvement with a lady librarian eleven years older than himself. This story was to reach its climax in that week's episodes in the studio and Frank Pemberton had been going over in his head the lines he was to deliver at rehearsal. Deep in thought he had been strolling up Quay Street to Granada's studios when a lady had detached herself from the shadows of the Opera House entrance, crossed the road and fallen into step with him.

'You don't know me, Mr Barlow,' she said, 'but we do have the same problem. My son's only nine years younger than this woman but we are just as worried about it as you are. What are you going to do about your Ken?'

Frank Barlow the character was probably the worst person on earth to have been asked that question but Frank Pemberton the actor was made of more considerate stuff.

At the same time he realized that the woman wanted a down-to-earth, *Coronation Street* answer. 'I know what I'd do,' he replied, 'but my wife says we've got to leave things be. They'll sort themselves out in the end. And come to think of it I suppose she's right.'

The woman had thanked him profusely and had left him on Granada's steps. It would be easy to dismiss her as a fantasist but it must be remembered that even now, when social workers are thick on the ground, most people are still left to solve their problems unaided. And when, on the television screen, they see people like themselves with the same troubles it becomes at least understandable that they should turn in that direction for help.

Generalization is dangerous at any time but I have studied the actor as a living organism at close quarters for many years and I would say that the majority of actors playing long-running parts offer a public image which is somewhere between their screen character and their true self. That way, on personal appearances, they can present to their fans all the well-known and well-loved facets of the character whilst offering a few tantalizing glimpses of the real person beneath. This behaviour is instinctive and stems from a pride in the character which they have created rather than a deliberate attempt to exploit that character. The peculiar relationship between artist and character, between Doris Speed and 'Annie Walker', Pat Phoenix and 'Elsie Tanner' or Violet Carson and 'Ena Sharples' is best explained by the artists themselves but it was partly created by a policy which was introduced very early in the programme's life. Writers were actively encouraged to mix with the artists both socially and inside the studios and it is amazing how many personal characteristics, picked up by sharp-eared scribes at tables in Granada's canteen, were infused subtly into the relevant characters. Not that the practice was universal. Some actors – those who were nearest in reality to the characters they portrayed – lent themselves naturally to this piracy. Others were light years from their characters. To take an example, the outwardly brash, extrovert Graham Haberfield and the shy, introverted 'Jerry Booth' he so brilliantly portrayed.

I first met the late Graham Haberfield in the early summer of 1962. The casting of single-episode parts was generally left to the director concerned but directors came and went and it was agreed that the producer should be responsible for the casting of any character with a long-term future. The casting of 'Jerry Booth' was my first step into this territory and I met Graham Haberfield as one of three candidates for the part in my office at Granada. Graham was playing out his last few weeks at Bristol Old Vic Drama School and was seeking his first professional job; I was looking for an apprentice for Len Fairclough. We chatted for a while. I described the shy, gauche but fanatically conscientious character we were seeking; he told me what he had been doing at Bristol. I had doubts. Whilst physically he was perfect for the role, his accent was disturbing. In fact he didn't seem to have one. I asked him why. 'They tried to knock it out of me at Drama School,' he explained apologetically. 'Did they succeed?' I asked. He shook his head and smiled and when I dug out a couple of copies of the first script in which the character appeared and read 'Len Fairclough' to his 'Jerry Booth' the natural Derbyshire accent complemented his physical appearance and it was patently obvious that there was no point in looking further.

Graham Haberfield was quick to prove my choice of casting had been right. He rapidly made the part his own and Jerry Booth became one of the *Street*'s most loved inhabitants. Like many of his colleagues he never totally came to terms with the split personality which his long-term contract demanded and his habit, as the floor manager was counting down the last few seconds to the start of recording, of lifting his eyes to the studio lights and shouting 'Goodbye, real world!' probably spoke volumes. He asked for a break in 1964 but within a few weeks he came

95

back to the fold and, happily accepted, he continued to delight his many *Coronation Street* fans for a further four years. In the early summer of 1968 however the itch began again and this time it was more serious. It was always difficult for a young actor to be content playing the same character year after year. After all, variety was what it was all about and insecurity was no stranger. He knew that he could never really prove himself as an actor unless he cut loose from 'Jerry Booth' and when he asked that his contract should not be renewed we could only fall in with his request and wish him well.

I joined him for a farewell drink on the night he left the *Street* but it was pretty obvious from the start that this was to be no happy occasion. He had already convinced himself that he was making the greatest mistake of his life and would never get another acting job as long as he lived. I tried to assure him that with his talent there would be no difficulty. He was a respected actor, I told him, and producers would be queuing up to employ him, but he saw himself as a stupid bum who had consigned himself to a disastrous future and nothing I could say would change his mind. There was only one thing to do – I had to lend some practical weight to my words – and as coincidence had it I was in a position to add that weight. Some weeks previously I had been asked to oversee – as executive producer – a short series of plays and one of them, a comedy by Jack Rosenthal intriguingly titled *There's a Hole in Your Dustbin, Delilah!* was approaching the casting stage. The play concerned the exploits of the gang of a Manchester refuse cart and the part of Winston, the crew-cut, football-mad young dustbinman was ready-made for Haberfield. However, although his name had been mentioned between Rosenthal, myself and Mike Apted, the director, there were other applicants to be considered. I decided to ignore them. Faced with the distraught actor, I resolved, inexcusably, to jump the gun. 'I will,' I said to him as he stared into a bleak future, 'prove to you how wrong you are. We

96

The line-up between rehearsals for the first and second episodes of *Coronation Street,* in December 1960.

Back row, left to right: IVAN BEAVIS, Harry Hewitt; JACK HOWARTH, Albert Tatlock; ERNST WALDER, Ivan Cheveski; PHILIP LOWRIE, Dennis Tanner; ALAN ROTHWELL, David Barlow; ARTHUR LESLIE, Jack Walker; WILLIAM CROASDALE, policeman; FRANK PEMBERTON, Frank Barlow; NOEL DYSON, Ida Barlow; MARGOT BRYANT, Minnie Caldwell.
Front row: DORIS SPEED, Annie Walker; BETTY ALBERGE, Florrie Lindley; ANNE CUNNINGHAM, Linda Cheveski; PATRICIA PHOENIX, Elsie Tanner; VIOLET CARSON, Ena Sharples; CHRISTINE HARGREAVES, Christine Hardman; WILLIAM ROACHE, Kenneth Barlow; PENNY RYDER, policewoman; PATRICIA SHAKESBY, Susan Cunningham; LYNNE CAROL, Martha Longhurst.

Survivors of episode one: cast, backroom boys and studio staff at the *Street*'s second birthday party.

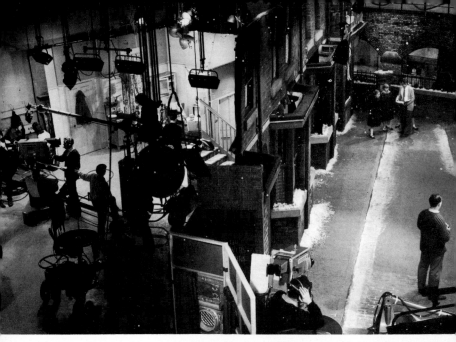

A historic photograph: three little girls receive their last instructions from the floor manager before *Coronation Street*'s very first shot.

The first of many confrontations. The absence of the hair-net and Ena's princess-line coat point to a rehearsal.

USELESS EUSTACE

220

JACK GREENALL

"... M GETTIN' SICK AND TIRED OF YOU LOOKIN' AT
UR WATCH AND SAYIN' 'AH, HAH, TIME FOR
CORONATION STREET'/ "

February '61 – a fractured gas main and the evacuation to the Glad Tidings Mission: one of the episodes re-shown during Granada's Silver Jubilee celebrations in May 1981.

A Jack Greenall cartoon from the *Daily Mirror*. One of the many reflecting the *Street*'s popularity over the years.
(Courtesy: Mirror Group Newspapers)

A farewell party for Harry Elton (between Bill Roache and Peter Adamson), the serial's first executive producer, before his return to Canada in 1963.

A lighter moment at a 1962 script conference. *L. to r.:* the late Harry Driver, Jack Rosenthal, the author, John Finch.

A familiar face in a familiar place. The late Sir Alfred Hitchcock on a visit to Granada, June 1964.

A front-step gossip. Anne Reid (Valerie Barlow) and Jean Alexander (Hilda Ogden) chat in the doorway of number 13.

Outside 10 Downing Street, March 1966. Sir Harold and Lady Wilson, aided by James Callaghan, wish the Australia party *bon voyage*.

On the Qantas V-JET. A toast to whatever lay ahead by the author, Arthur Leslie, Doris Speed and Pat Phoenix.

The scene outside Adelaide town hall. One of the tour party's many official engagements.

Hilda Ogden helps daughter Irma (Sandra Gough) take over the corner shop while husband Stan (Bernard Youens) indulges his favourite hobby. In 1967 the *Street* frontage was still built in the studio.

The *grandes dames* – Ena and Annie.

Another shot from 1967. Elsie Tanner and Len Fairclough (Peter Adamson) stroll down the studio-built street.

Annie, Jack and Ena
side-titled in
Mandarin, ready for
Singapore.

Three of the
founder-members. A
1968 scene with
Albert, Elsie and Ken.

Champagne and a birthday cake. The Variety Club's lunch at the London Savoy to mark ten years of *Coronation Street*.

Between takes: Anne Reid, Bill Roache, Peter Adamson and Pat Phoenix relax during a recording session.

1971 and Albert's still laying down the law to Hilda and Ena.

On the new outside lot, 1974. Note how the cobblestones have changed direction from the earlier studio layout.

More advice for Elsie. Violet Carson and Pat Phoenix ignoring a mass of electronics in a 1977 episode.

A happy group in London for the Pye/Writers' Guild award ceremony, 1979.

Back row, l. to r.: PETER DUDLEY, Bert Tilsley; MADGE HINDLE, Renee Roberts; CHERYL MURRAY, Suzie Birchall; JOHNNY BRIGGS, Mike Baldwin; LYNNE PERRIE, Ivy Tilsley; LAWRENCE MULLIN, Steve Fisher; FRED FEAST, Fred Gee; BRYAN MOSLEY, Alf Roberts; JEAN ALEXANDER, Hilda Ogden; GEOFFREY HUGHES, Eddie Yeats; BETTY DRIVER, Betty Turpin; WILLIAM ROACHE, Ken Barlow; HELEN WORTH, Gail Tilsley
Front row, l. to r.: THELMA BARLOW, Mavis Riley; JULIE GOODYEAR, Bet Lynch; SIR JOHN BETJEMAN; DORIS SPEED, Annie Walker; JACK HOWARTH, Albert Tatlock; PATRICIA PHOENIX, Elsie Tanner.

An off-duty visit to the street by Julie Goodyear (Bet Lynch) and Peter Adamson.

Stan in trouble again. Hilda asks some searching questions about Mrs Webb (played by Eileen Kennally) while Elsie looks on.

At the Variety Club, 1980. Doris Speed and Bill Podmore accept the Club's Silver Heart from Dickie Henderson.

A gaggle of producers at the *Street*'s 20th birthday party. *L. to r.:* Derek Granger, the author, Harry (Stuart) Latham, Bill Podmore, Howard Baker and Richard Everitt.

Granada executives, the production team and cast of *Coronation Street* with their guests at a dinner to mark the serial's 2000th episode.

David Frost and Russell Harty join in a tribute to the serial at the 1981 BAFTA awards.

TAM'S TOP 20 PROGRAMMES

	Programme		Homes Viewing		Programme		Hom View
1	Coronation Street (Mon.)	(Gran.)	8,868,000	11	Bruce Forsyth Show	(ATV)	5,831,
2	Coronation Street (Wed.)	(Gran.)	8,625,000	12	A Lily in Little India	(ATV)	5,588,
3	Dead Letter	(ABC)	7,289,000		Linda Came Today	(ATV)	5,588,
4	Val Parnell's Sunday Show	(ATV)	6,924,000	14	Emergency Ward 10 (Tues.)	(ATV)	5,467,
5	Malgret	(BBC)	6,560,000	15	The Avengers	(ABC)	5,388,
	No Hiding Place	(AR)	6,560,000	16	Zero 1	(BBC)	5,345,
	Emergency Ward 10 (Fri.)	(ATV)	6,560,000	17	Here's Harry	(BBC)	5,224,
8	Double Your Money	(AR)	6,195,000		Z Cars	(BBC)	5,224,
9	Take Your Pick	(AR)	6,185,000		Sportsview	(BBC)	5,224,
10	Winning Widows	(ATV)	5,884,000	20	Take a Letter	(Gran.)	5,081,

The top twenty programmes as listed in the *Television Mail* on 26 October 1962.

TVRatings top 20 network television programmes produced for **Jictar** by **AGB**

The Network 'Top Twenty' and area 'Top Tens' are the copyright of JICTAR and any subsequent reproduction, in whole or in part, must contain a reference to JICTAR.

WEEK ENDING 29TH JUNE 1980

		Originating Programme Company	ITV Areas	Individuals Viewing Millions
1	CORONATION STREET (WED 25 JUN)	GRANADA	ALL	14.65
2	CORONATION STREET (MON 23 JUN)	GRANADA	ALL	14.00
3	HERE COMES SUMMER	GRANADA	ALL	12.85
4	CROSSROADS (WED 25 JUN)	ATV	ALL	12.75
5	WINNER TAKES ALL	YORKSHIRE	ALL	12.60
6	CAN WE GET ON NOW, PLEASE?	GRANADA	ALL	12.55
7	THE KRYPTON FACTOR	GRANADA	ALL	12.30
8	WORLD IN ACTION	GRANADA	ALL	12.10
8=	DON'T JUST SIT THERE	YORKSHIRE	ALL	12.10
10	STARSKY AND HUTCH	BBC	ALL	12.05
11	THE KILLERS	BBC	ALL	12.00
12	THE OTHER 'ARF	ATV	ALL	11.80
13	THE CUCKOO WALTZ	GRANADA	ALL EXC S.W.	11.50
14	CROSSROADS (TUE 24 JUN)	ATV	ALL EXC LCS	11.40
15	NINE O'CLOCK NEWS (FRI 27 JUNE)	BBC	ALL	11.30
16	ROBIN'S NEST	THAMES	ALL	11.10
17	THE MALLENS	GRANADA	ALL	10.75
18	EMMERDALE FARM (TUE 24 JUN)	YORKSHIRE	ALL	10.35
19	RETURN OF THE SAINT	ATV	ALL	10.20
20	NINE O'CLOCK NEWS (MON 23 JUN)	BBC	ALL	10.15

The top twenty in the JICTAR ratings for th week ending 29 June 1980.
(Reproduction authorized by the Join Industry Committee fo Television Advertisin Research)

were going to ring your agent next Monday and offer you a good part in a new Jack Rosenthal play.' At first he didn't believe me but eventually I managed to convince him that the part was his and he went home a happier man. Which was more than I could say for myself.

The following morning I rang Jack Rosenthal and Mike Apted and confessed my sin. Amazingly they shared the same reaction. Not anger that I had pre-empted their right of choice but relief that Haberfield had accepted the part. Secretly – even from each other – they had made him their first choice and they were delighted that this part, at least, was cast. My relief was enormous but things were to get even better. Haberfield revelled in the part of Winston and when, a few months later, a comedy series called *The Dustbinmen*, based on the original play, went into production at Granada's studios, Graham Haberfield was one of the few actors to retain his original part and to play it with great success throughout the series.

Graham Haberfield went on to enrich a variety of roles both for the BBC and for the independent companies. His premature death was a great shock and a loss not only to his friends and colleagues in television but to a wide audience who were denied his considerable talent.

To the acting profession insecurity is an occupational hazard. This is something of a paradox as the actor deliberately seeks insecurity as part of his life. Ideally he should tick off the years playing dustmen and belted earls, heroes and villains, never knowing when the next job is coming but somehow always finding one. Only a few live this halcyon existence. Arthur Lowe, who gave such wonderful service to *Coronation Street* as Leonard Swindley, the pompous little draper, is still leaping from success to success. Jack Howarth, the *Street*'s Albert Tatlock, has hardly known a day's 'resting' (the actor's euphemism for unemployment) since the beginning of the twentieth century! For the vast majority of their professional colleagues, however, the picture is far bleaker. They must endure long periods of

97

inactivity between parts and it is only fair that they should be amongst the small proportion of the self-employed who are allowed to draw unemployment benefit. Curiously, however, the landing of a long-running role does not necessarily cure this feeling of insecurity. Only the fears are different. Now it is not 'When will I get another job?' but 'How long will this one last?' The danger now is that having learned to live well, having taken on financial commitments, a change of fashion or the axing of a programme can not only send the unhappy actor back into obscurity but send him there with his pockets full of unpaid bills. Add to this the pressures which have already been talked about in these pages and it is small wonder that some actors and actresses, subjecting themselves to public scrutiny week after week should seek some form of comfort. And the most readily available is drink.

Peter Adamson has readily told the story of his continuing fight against alcoholism but it may be of interest to view his problem from another angle. The character of Len Fairclough was formed in the first few weeks of *Coronation Street* mainly as a social partner for Harry Hewitt who had been a central character since episode one. So assertively was the character played by Peter Adamson that it rapidly achieved an importance of its own and by the beginning of 1964 the character led the male defence against the monstrous battalions of the *Street*'s women. But the pressures of those four lime-lit years had taken their toll on Peter Adamson. He was, although he didn't know it at the time, in the second stage of alcoholism.

Looking back on those uneasy months it is difficult to understand how the programme maintained any semblance of quality. Peter Adamson's drunkenness hung like an albatross around the programme's neck and my responsibilities as producer were beginning to weigh very heavily indeed. Matters were made worse by the fact that I had known Peter in happier days. I knew him to be not only a dedicated and talented actor but a caring family man and because of this what should have been the simple expedient of sacking him became a very difficult prospect indeed. There was another reason – impersonal but none the less important. The programme was planned almost three months ahead and Len Fairclough was constantly included in that forward planning. At each story conference during this difficult period we would include the character in our projected plots, hoping that Peter Adamson's problem would miraculously disappear. This was wishful thinking at its most stupid and it rapidly became evident as matters grew worse that drastic action needed to be taken. The situation had been prolonged, strangely enough, by the attitude of Peter's colleagues. Such is the cameraderie of the acting profession that the vast majority of his colleagues tried their damnedest to cover up for Peter. In the studio they would mask his deficiencies by their own performances. Outside they would organize a rota to ensure that he was left alone as little as possible. And whilst Peter was in the studio his friends would, at regular intervals, search his dressing-room and dispose of any liquor they might find. But this defence, well meaning though it was, couldn't last forever and the strain was beginning to tell on us all.

In July 1964 I decided that the time had come when Peter Adamson had to be written out of *Coronation Street*. The question remained, when was this suspension to begin. If immediately it meant that three months hard work of planning and scriptwriting would go to waste and a great deal of effort would need to be put into the re-shaping of those episodes. On the other hand if we were secretly to write him out from that point but to play through the stories we had plotted it would mean committing ourselves to a further three months of tribulation. There was, I decided, a middle way. I would tell Peter of his suspension immediately but the suspension itself would not begin until we had played out those stories we had planned. Moreover, the length of the suspension (which would be at least three months), would depend on his behaviour during his remaining weeks with the programme. He would be suspended without pay but Granada would meet any medical fees for the treatment of his complaint. Suspension without pay, though apparently harsh, was an integral part of my hopeful plan. Peter, as I have already said, was a caring husband and father and I concluded, rightly or wrongly, that as long as his alcoholism only hit him he had no real cause to fight it but when it began to attack the family purse there could well be an incentive to start some kind of treatment.

I took my plan to Cecil Bernstein and talked it over with him. He was doubtful that the long period between the threat of suspension and the suspension itself could be anything other than a disadvantage but he understood the problems which would be caused by Peter's instant dismissal from the programme and gave my idea his blessing. Not that I was in any way certain that the scheme would work. Anyone who has lived or worked with an alcoholic will know the volatile nature of the victim and the thought of Peter's possible reactions to the plan was a frightening one.

The following day I sent for Peter and told him what I planned to do. His immediate reaction, as I recall it, was to call me a crafty bastard. At the time I didn't know why but later when his treatment was under way and I went to visit him he confessed that he had always banked on Granada's reluctance to tear up three months of planning and get rid of him. The cunning which leads alcoholics to hide their bottles in inaccessible places had led him to believe that his financial future at least was secure and the shattering of this belief was in fact the first step towards his recovery. It would have been much better for my peace of mind had I known this earlier. As it was I could only wait for the days to show success or failure.

As the weeks went by it became obvious that whether by good luck or good judgement – and it didn't matter which – my plan was meeting with some success. Through the help of his many friends and the advice of a trusted specialist, the old Peter Adamson began to emerge. By the end of the probationary period Peter was well on his way to winning the first battle. Again I found myself faced with a dilemma. It was clear that my action had had the desired effect but, now that Peter's improvement was obvious, would it be fair to implement my threat and carry out the proposed suspension? I decided, for two reasons, to carry through my original plan. Firstly it would allow Peter to undergo full-time treatment, in hospital if necessary. Secondly, Peter still needed the discipline of strong decisions and had he been granted a free pardon and allowed to carry on working it might, in his still troubled mind, have been interpreted as a sign of weakness and could have had a disastrous effect. The suspension began in early October and three months later Peter Adamson rejoined the programme. Today, seventeen years on, he is still with us. Although he continues to play the hard-drinking, sometimes drunken Len Fairclough, Peter Adamson is winning his personal fight against alcoholism. He and his family are content again, as are the millions who enjoy his undoubted talent. And that's a happy outcome in anyone's book.

Although it would be wrong to single out any individual for particular praise it would be equally unfair not to make special mention of those artists who have been with the programme since its inception. They had to create not only the people of the *Street* but the style of acting which has characterized the programme over the years. On the credit side they enjoyed the magic of those early months as the show grew from its modest beginnings to a fully-networked leader of the Top Ten but this is no more than their due when one realizes that the metamorphosis was largely attributable to them. No one who can remember Ena's fearsome eye and that machine-gun delivery, Mrs Tanner's despairing glance into the flyblown mirror and that heartfelt 'Eh, Elsie, you're ready for the knacker's yard!', the realism of Annie and Jack in the Rovers Return or the class war fought out by the Barlows and Uncle Albert can help but appreciate the contribution made by Violet Carson, Pat Phoenix, Doris Speed, William Roache and Jack Howarth, all of whom are still with the programme as I write. These survivors from the first episode were soon joined by Peter Adamson (Len Fairclough), Eileen Derbyshire (Emily Bishop) and Brian Mosley (Alf Roberts), actors and creations which the *Street* has been fortunate to keep during its long life.

If it was difficult to step into the unknown at the start of a new twice-weekly serial it was scarcely less hard to make one's mark in an established, well-loved show. Many young actors (and not a few experienced ones) have confessed their nervousness when they walk into the rehearsal room to begin their first stint on the *Street*. And why not? Whilst many are called, few are chosen and although it is true that no *Street* artist (particularly one who has made an impression) is ever wholly forgotten, only rarely do they stay to join the élite company of contract artists. *Coronation Street* never looks first for the actor. We never say 'We must have X in the show, let's think up a character for him.' The search always starts for the character and the contract is won by the artist who can give the production team the character they want, which isn't always immediately apparent. Being a non-stop, twice-weekly show, we are able to audition on the screen. Many an apparent 'bit' part is being closely scrutinized for a long future. If it doesn't work, we say 'goodbye!'; if it does, the artist is invited to join the contract cast.

Len Fairclough needed a woman in his life and Barbara Knox filled every fibre of Rita Littlewood, the character we wanted. Rita, in turn, needed a woman to play against in the newsagent's shop and Mavis, created by Thelma Barlow, filled the gap perfectly. Houses fall empty, need to be filled. Into number thirteen move, inevitably, the Ogdens. And after a few weeks of Bernard Youens and Jean Alexander as the ill-starred Stan and Hilda it is patently obvious that they are here to stay for ever. And staying with them, their 'bin-man' lodger Eddie Yeats – hilariously – and often poignantly – interpreted by Geoffrey Hughes. In the Rovers Return, the landlord has died and son, Billy (Kenneth Farrington), though destined to make many a return appearance has left for pastures new. Unknown to the viewing public a series of on-screen auditions take place and from the welter of bar-staff, Betty Turpin (played by Betty Driver), Bet Lynch (Julie Goodyear) and Fred Gee (Fred Feast) rise from the ruck and make the positions firmly their own. And not only in the Rovers Return. All of them take centre-stage in their own stories outside the pub, particularly the irrepressible barmaid, Bet. Another year or two pass and a factory opens on the other side of the street.

Who moves in? Johnny Briggs, Lynne Perrie, Elizabeth Dawn and Helene Palmer put flesh on to the bones of Mike Baldwin, Ivy, Vera and Ida, and the problem is solved. And when yet another house falls vacant, Ivy moves in with husband Bert (Peter Dudley) and son Brian (Christopher Quinten) and the Tilsley family begins to put down roots.

Not all new characters are brought in to fill specific roles. Sometimes our needs are far more general. The show may find itself short of young girls and from the thousands of aspiring young actresses, Anne Kirkbride and Helen Worth give us Deirdre and Gail and weave their characters unerringly into the romantic fabric of the *Street*. Or a chance remark at a story conference – 'We haven't got any kids!' – sets the stage for the arrival of Tracy Langton, played with huge relish and high professionalism by Christabel Finch almost from the moment of birth!

Nothing excites the TV journalist more than a death in *Coronation Street*. Even the pressmen themselves find it hard to explain why. They know from the letters they receive that their readership dislikes such disclosures, much preferring to be surprised by the programme events, but in spite of this, they cannot resist spoiling the suspense. 'I don't know why we do it,' one television reporter confessed to me. 'All I know is that if *I* didn't blow the story someone else would.'

When Renée Roberts was 'killed' in a car crash in July 1980, one paper, blowing the story a couple of weeks before transmission with pictures of the accident from what we fondly thought to be a secret location, boastfully referred to the death as being 'exclusively forecast in the *Daily Mirror*'. It's difficult to credit such fantasy. Braving shot and shell to report the Afghanistan war is one thing, paying a 'mole' for fictional information which, when printed, is going to infuriate most of his readers is another. I have been told that the going rate for such information is £200. What a strange world it is! On the one hand the pressman is actively encouraged by his employers to operate in this manner; on the other, the 'mole', if uncovered, would almost certainly lose his job and find it difficult to work in television again.

The Press apart, screen 'killings' invariably cause heartache within the production team. Only on the rarest occasion is a character's death the fault of the actor concerned. There are times when, for personal or family reasons an artist asks to be released from his or her contract but this is standard procedure and cannot be described as anyone's fault. Usually characters – and I mean characters, not artists – are dropped from the programme and their creators' contracts not renewed through the failure of the production team to find suitable stories. Some characters – Ena Sharples and Albert Tatlock spring to mind – are 'lamppost' figures, a part of the scenery of such streets who earn their keep by being there. Others spark off a multitude of stories or are easily and profitably involved in the stories of others. Yet others have sat uneasily between, their actions repetitious, their use limited and it is this group which, over the years, have been written out of the show.

But, whatever the reason for dropping the character may be, death is always the last option. Successive producers of *Coronation Street* have come to realize that the ability to bring back old friends who have not been seen for ten, fifteen, perhaps twenty years, is a tremendous asset which adds enormously to the 'reality' of the serial. For no other reason it is vastly preferable to let a character walk out of the *Street* rather than be carried out feet first.

Whether or not a character should die depends largely on two differing sets of circumstances, one personal to the actor, one pertinent to the programme. An actor can become so identified with his *Street* role that months, even years after leaving he or she is still ignored by other producers. 'Old So-and-so?' they'll say. 'Isn't he still in *Coronation Street*?' When Ivan Beavis, the *Street*'s Harry Hewitt for its opening years, found that months after leaving the show outside producers still thought of him as a *Street* inhabitant, he came to Jack Rosenthal, the producer of the time, and asked to be 'killed off'. Jack, sensitive to Ivan's unhappy position, arranged for Harry to reappear as a guest at Steve and Elsie Tanner's wedding and, on leaving, to die under his car as a badly-fixed jack collapsed. Only then did Ivan Beavis start to work again.

When the actor playing Ray Langton left *Coronation Street* at his own request there was no necessity for the character to die or for his screen wife and daughter, Deirdre and Tracy to leave with him. It was perfectly consistent with the character of Ray that he should desert his family to take a better-paid job in Holland and this is what happened when Neville Buswell was released from his contract. When, however, Stephen Hancock (playing Ernest Bishop) left the show it was obvious that the only way he could go was via the Pearly Gates. A lay preacher and a dutiful husband, it would have dealt a severe blow to the sanctity of marriage had he run off with a disco dancer. Why, some may ask, wasn't he consigned to a sanatorium after a bout of delicate coughing? Unfortunately it's never that simple.

Invalids tend to be an embarrassment if they're not visited regularly and if the departed actor is as busy as he hopes to be it is always difficult to bring him back to lie in his hospital bed at a mutually convenient time.

Stephen Hancock was by no means the first to suffer under this philosophy. When Noel Dyson (Ida Barlow) joined the cast in 1960 she made it clear that she had no intention of staying longer than nine months and a couple of months before her exit she came to me and asked if I had decided the manner of her going. 'I'm afraid you're going to have to die,' I told her. She wasn't surprised. A model wife and mother, there was no way Ida Barlow would have left her beloved family other than by illness or death. And illness, as I have explained, was impractical. She made one request. 'I'd rather Ida didn't die from anything to do with her heart,' she said.

I put her mind at rest. 'I had a double-decker bus in mind,' I said.

'Marvellous!' she replied, and that was that.

The constant demand to appear before their public is one of the penalties to be paid by the *Coronation Street* contract artists. However they all realize that the danger signals are alight when this demand ceases and they perform their duties with fortitude and a brave smile. Some enjoy personal appearances more than others, some see the work as necessary moonlighting though Heaven knows they all do a tiring week's work.

Let no one imagine that appearing amongst one's public is a dignified affair. I have been nearer to death at personal appearances than ever I was during the war – and *I* was an innocent, unrecognized bystander.

One such riot took place in the summer of 1961, when Sheila Atha, the *Street*'s stage manager invited her friends from the cast to her forthcoming wedding in Wallasey, Cheshire. Meant to be a quiet affair it escalated into a State occasion when the cast accepted and the Press leaked the details in advance. The local police were worried. Could special stickers be issued to all the guests for display on their cars, please? Would we use the emergency car parks commandeered for the day? Back in Manchester we took these arrangements with a pinch of salt but when the day came and we were escorted by motor cycle police from the outskirts of Wallasey, through massed cheering crowds to the Town Hall where the civil ceremony was to be held, we realized that without this organization bride would never have met groom that day. The ceremony over, I came down the Town Hall's main stairway with an awe stricken Town Clerk. 'The Queen was here last year,' he said. 'It was nothing like this.'

The reception was held at a restaurant on Wallasey's central roundabout and the crowds below, waiting for another glimpse of those famous faces, grew into a considerable traffic hazard. My wife and I had brought along Jack Howarth, the *Street*'s Albert Tatlock, and his wife, Betty, and we decided to wait until the rest of the guests had gone and the crowds had cleared before starting for home. We were enjoying a quiet drink when a police inspector joined us. 'Could I ask you to leave, sir?' he said to Jack.

'Why?' asked Jack, not unnaturally. There were still crowds down on the streets, explained the inspector, and they wouldn't go away until Jack had left.

'Go on!' said Jack. 'They don't know I'm up here!'

'Don't they?' said the inspector. 'Some joker's made a list and yours is the only name as hasn't been crossed off yet. It'd help if you'd go, sir. I'd like to get the traffic moving again.'

I am still, after twenty years, amazed at the quality of performance in the *Street*. It stems from an easy camaraderie which transfers itself from rehearsal room to screen. Much of the friendly relationship – and the less friendly detachment – to be observed on the screen are reflections of true working rapport or lack of it. Whilst it would be quite wrong to describe the contract cast of *Coronation Street* as a seething hot-bed of envy and passion it would be equally wrong to say that the contract artists love each other to distraction and cannot see enough of each other. The simple in-between truth is that, emotionally motivated people though they all may be, they form a normal work force, working, for the most part perfectly happily, to make the best product they can. Perhaps, on reflection, they are not a normal work force. Ask artists to work into the night to perfect a scene and the vast majority will agree without hesitation. They have not yet learned to work within all the strictures of modern Trade Unionism and it looks now as if they never will.

Perhaps the serial would not reap such a rich harvest from its actors if it didn't sow such good seed. If it had asked Pat Phoenix to play merely the *femme fatale*, Jean Alexander to give us nothing but a downtrodden housewife and Julie Goodyear to concentrate solely on the barmaid with the heart of gold it would have been a lesser show. But it didn't. Its demands are much greater. It asks every contract artist to make 'em laugh, make 'em cry and make 'em feel every emotion in between. That the cast responds in such a talented fashion is a powerful reason for the show's artistic success.

CHAPTER NINE

'They're not like us, you know, foreigners. They're
er . . . you know, foreign!'

Stan Ogden

By the end of 1965 *Coronation Street* had established itself as a
firm favourite far beyond the shores of the British Isles. If it
had been a mystery to its producers that such 'foreign'
areas as East Anglia and Scotland should take the programme to their bosoms it was even more baffling that the
events of a Lancashire backstreet should touch a chord in
the hearts of tribesmen in northern Nigeria, Thais in Bang-
kok and the Malays, Indians and Chinese of Singapore.
We reasoned – and correspondence from these areas supported our reasoning – that there are Elsie Tanners everywhere and that each community of whatever colour,
creed or size stands in fear of its Ena Sharples. Some years
later when the *Street* was enjoying a brief showing in New
York a Brooklyn man wrote to me saying that every single
character in the show lived in his apartment block.

Those countries who bought the serial and who did not
have English as a mother tongue were, naturally enough,
faced with language problems. Single programmes – plays,
for instance – are normally dubbed, that is to say a new
soundtrack is prepared in the language of the transmitting
country. This method however – as anyone who has seen
a dubbed film will know – has its drawbacks. The dialogue
is often distorted to follow the lip movements of the actor
with sometimes hilarious results. More important, dubbing
is an expensive operation. For a single play or a major
documentary this objection is relatively unimportant but
the dubbing of a serial such as *Coronation Street* becomes a
difficult and disproportionately costly exercise. Sub-titling

therefore became the most popular means of bringing the *Street* dialogue to the foreign viewer. Even here there were difficulties. *Coronation Street* is not written or performed in the Queen's English but in a strong and unashamed Lancashire dialect and the job of the translator was no easy one.

There were other local problems. Although English is one of Singapore's four official languages the majority of the population uses Mandarin Chinese and to meet that majority demand the programme was sub-titled in that language. Or, to be more correct, side-titled as the Chinese characters run up the left-hand side of the screen. This, however, was not enough. Whilst the wealthier residents speak either Chinese or English many of the inhabitants of Singapore's Coronation Streets speak Tamil. If Tamil sub-titles were to be added to the Mandarin Chinese side-titles there wouldn't be much of the Rovers Return left unobscured, so the easy answer was unacceptable. The solution, when found, was ingenious. One of Singapore's many radio channels became the Tamil voice of *Coronation Street* and the Tamil speaker sat at home watching the show on his television set and listening to a radio voice giving a running commentary on the passing scene. I would very much have liked to have seen this in action but when, eventually, my *Coronation Street* travels took me to Singapore it was for the briefest of airport stops and the chance was lost.

Happily Singapore was an extreme case and most non-English-speaking countries get by with simple sub-titles. On reflection perhaps 'simple' is an unfair word to use. Translation of the Lancashire dialect into sub-titles which tell the story, establish the characters and yet do not detract from the enjoyment of the programme as a whole is an exacting, painstaking and largely unrewarding process. No matter how much care is taken there are always unseen pitfalls which catch the interpreter unaware. I remember showing a visiting Dutch sub-titler round Granada's studios. He had come over from VARA TV who transmitted the *Street* from Hilversum, Holland's radio and television city and it was natural enough that our set should figure on his itinerary. As we walked around the empty studio, in and out of the Rovers Return, through Minnie's living-room and into the Ogden's kitchen, Mynheer spotted the corner shop. 'May I go in?' he asked.

'Certainly,' I told him. I expected him to enter the set through the 'fourth wall', the open end where the cameras and sound booms cluster but he did no such thing. He edged his way between the corner shop 'flats' and the neighbouring set and entered the shop as if he were a customer. The bell, tripped by the opening door, tinkled. The Dutchman turned, looked up at the bell and sadly shook his head. 'That damned bell,' he said in impeccable English. And then he explained. Readers of sub-titles are easily distracted, he believes, and it is his practice to insert his titles on the screen only in moments of silence. Normally a reading of the script helped him but not in that 'damned corner shop'. He would select a quiet moment, punch-up the sub-title and just as the reader was half way through the line of Dutch, 'ping' would go the bell and bang would go the concentration. I had to admit to him that I couldn't muster much sympathy for his predicament. All my concern, I said, was for the poor Malay family in its wooden hut on the banks of the Singapore River, watching on a third-hand TV set the strange antics of a bunch of Lancashire folk, trying to ignore the Mandarin characters which obscured one of Bet Lynch's salient features and at the same time striving desperately to follow the plot as the Tamil-speaking radio commentator competed with the drumming of equatorial rain on the corrugated iron roof.

Although Len Fairclough and Minnie Caldwell may have been recognizable characters on the Nigerian plateau or the shores of the Zuyder Zee the warmest response to the programme came from the Commonwealth. Not only was English the mother-tongue of Australia, New Zealand and, to a large extent, Canada but most of the inhabitants of those countries had family roots in Britain. And, as many of the emigrants had fled from decaying industrial areas, there was a strong nostalgia for the clustered terraced streets of the North-West of England. Many an Australian child had been told by parent or grandparent of fish and chips, local pubs, trips to Blackpool, cotton mills and cold, rainy days. Of Uncle Ted and Auntie Alice who still lived in Accrington. And Cousin Jimmy who actually went to see Manchester United play every other Saturday. With all this going for it, it was not surprising that *Coronation Street* took hold of the hearts of the English-speaking Commonwealth. Nor was it unexpected when requests began to arrive at Granada's Manchester headquarters for the *Street* to 'tour' these distant yet familiar lands.

The most insistent of these requests came early in 1966 from the Australian commercial network which had been transmitting the show twice a week for three years to avid audiences in all of the continent's major cities. There had been tempting offers in the past but the most important question had always been – how would any outside activity affect the programme shown to the British audience twice a week? If it was seen or even thought to be detrimental the invitation was politely declined. On this occasion, after due debate, it was decided that a four-week tour by a maximum of three members of the cast could be arranged without any serious damage. Once this decision was made events moved quickly. Telex machines chattered and international telephone wires hummed as Granada in Britain and the Australian network comprising Channel 9 in Sydney, Melbourne and Adelaide ironed out the details of the coming tour.

This may be an opportune moment to describe, for reasons which will soon become obvious, the essential differences between an executive producer and a producer. At that time the *Street* had one of each. Peter Eckersley, who had been one of the serial's finest writers and was to become Granada's Head of Drama, was producing the show.

I was executive producer. It was Peter's job to look after the week-by-week running of the programme, to hire directors, assist those directors in casting new artists, hire and commission writers, determine with his storyline writers the composition of future episodes and supervise the eventual rehearsal and making of those episodes. On the face of it there didn't seem much left for an executive producer to do but that was far from being the truth. I had to concern myself creatively with longer-term planning and the search for new writers and major storylines, diplomatically with labour relations in a greatly varied community, helpfully with the personal problems of that team and officially with programme policy. Did we, for instance, believe that our contract artists should be allowed to do radio work whilst under contract to the programme? It will be seen from these duties that the *Street* was largely self-governing and that practically every decision concerning the show could be made either by its producer or its executive producer without recourse to the management.

Certain decisions however remained firmly with the management although the executive producer's views were always sought. To fly the programme's flag in Australia had been a Board decision and I insisted that the choice of the lucky artists should be another. This could be seen as 'chickening-out' in some quarters and I have to say to those who might have thought that way that they were probably right up to a point. But it must be remembered that this was something not only special but incapable of being shared by all our contract cast and we had always believed in *Coronation Street* that sharing was the name of the game. At that time the regular contract cast numbered twenty-three and most of them, I knew, wanted to go. The tour schedule made a great deal of air travel necessary and the one or two artists who refused to fly automatically ruled themselves out but still twenty names remained from which only three could be chosen.

It was at this point in the general discussion that I put on

113

my diplomat's hat and suggested that the management should choose our three representatives. I argued that as I would be forced to work closely with the entire cast perhaps long after the tour was finished it would be unwise for me to be involved in anything that could even smack of favouritism. The management agreed and a few days later I was told that the party would consist of myself (which was, to say the least, unexpected), Norman Frisby (Granada's Press Officer) and, from the cast, Doris Speed, Pat Phoenix and the late and sadly-missed Arthur Leslie. The management's preference turned out to be admirable though this was small comfort to the losers. It's not enough to say that actors are human – they're more human than most of us – and I didn't blame them in the least for feeling disappointed. As has been said before in this book, there has never been a star system as such in *Coronation Street* and it was the Press rather than Granada which 'created' one or two 'stars' for no better reason than to give themselves a kind of shorthand. At a Press conference called to cover the impending trip to Australia I was asked if the show could carry on without its 'stars'. I rebuked the questioner, gently. 'There are no stars in *Coronation Street*,' I said.

This time it was my turn to be rebuked, both gently and politely. 'What Mr Kershaw means,' said Pat Phoenix, 'is that we're *all* stars!'

The Australian tour was due to start from Heathrow on 17 March 1966 and a great deal had to be done in the few weeks between decision and departure. It seemed, too, that the social events were to begin quite a time before the Qantas Jetliner's wheels left the tarmac. Press conferences were held, both in London and Manchester. The tour party were invited by Cecil Bernstein to lunch with the Australian High Commissioner and his wife, a couple of charming Anglophiles. His Excellency, disturbed by Australia's drift towards republicanism, urged us to carry the flag. Nor was he alone. Prime Minister Harold Wilson invited us to 10 Downing Street.

The Labour Government, elected in 1964, had seen its slender majority of five eroded and a General Election had been called for 31 March. Cynical political observers, on hearing of the *Street* invitation, pointed out that a friendly liaison with Elsie Tanner and Jack and Annie Walker would hardly damage the party's popular vote but for our part, being as human as the next bloke, we were delighted to be asked.

The party of four – Norman Frisby had flown on ahead to meet his fellow-Pressmen in Australia – met at Golden Square, Granada's London HQ, at 11.30 on the morning of Monday, 13 March. The reception at Downing Street was timed for noon and at 11.40 a massive, black Daimler limousine purred into the Square. A last-minute cosmetic fuss from the ladies of the party and we were on our way. The traffic was light and it was still only seven minutes to twelve when we reached the turn to Downing Street. 'Stop here on Whitehall for a few minutes,' I told the driver and then, turning to my three charges I added, prophetically as it turned out, 'Right, five minutes break! Get the fags out!' There was an immediate scuffle for cigarettes and lighters. I was to give up smoking for ever not three months later but at this time I was an addict and I eagerly joined Pat and Doris and Arthur in a nerve-soothing cigarette. One of the greatest discoveries of my adult life, when I did finally kick the habit, was to find that I had never really needed what I had long believed was the help and comfort of tobacco. After years of kidding myself, as I sat in front of my typewriter, that the next line of dialogue would only come if I lit up a cigarette, it was wonderful to discover how wrong I had been. But that morning in Whitehall the nicotine still soothed. After all, one didn't meet Prime Ministers on their home ground every day of the week. The cigarettes extinguished and the dashboard clock showing one minute to twelve, I asked the driver to move on.

We were quite unprepared for the crowds. The morning papers had splashed the visit but the normal Downing

Street gathering had been heavily supplemented, not only by *Street* fans but, it seemed, by every Press photographer in London. The atmosphere was festive and shouts of 'You tell 'em, Elsie!' and 'Give him one of your looks, Annie!' greeted us as we left the car. I knocked at the door and we were invited inside by a smiling young personal assistant who led us past the household staff lining the narrow entrance hall and upstairs to a small reception room. The general effect was one of mild decay and I shared Arthur Leslie's surprise when he leaned across and whispered 'I thought they'd just spent a million pounds on the place?' It was difficult to see where the money had gone.

After a short wait we were guided to a first-floor drawing-room where the Prime Minister made us welcome and introduced us to his wife, to Jim Callaghan who as Chancellor and neighbour had 'nipped in from next door' and to his Press Secretary. The reception was warm and the ice soon broke as we arranged ourselves in a hollow square around the Adam fireplace. Mr Callaghan, Arthur and myself faced the Prime Minister, strategically placed between Pat and Doris with Mrs Wilson and the Press Secretary facing the fireplace. Sherry arrived and conversation flowed but in spite of the friendly atmosphere I could sense a tautness, a nervousness not only in Pat, Doris and Arthur but in myself as well. I was racking my brains as to what might be wrong when the Prime Minister lit his pipe. Realization struck. We were all dying for a cigarette. I looked for confirmation of my theory and spotted it in Doris's twitching fingers and Arthur's agonized looks at the smoke curling from the Prime Minister's briar. Patience, I told myself – someone will hand the cigarettes round soon. But no one did. Ten minutes of agony passed.

I took my courage in both hands, pulled out a rather battered packet of Player's Gold Leaf and rose to my feet. 'Cigarette, Mr Chancellor?' The offer was refused. 'Arthur?' Arthur bestowed on me a look of pure gratitude, made a wild grab and took three. Two went back into the packet and I continued my trip around the illustrious feet. 'Mrs Wilson?' Again no. Likewise for the Press Secretary. On to Doris who accepted my offer with shaking hands and a merry trill of gratitude. 'Prime Minister? Oh, of course, you're smoking!' And on to Pat who breathed 'Thank God' as she took the proffered cigarette. From that moment relaxation became complete but, strangely enough, I was allowed to repeat the operation twice before we left. I've often wondered why. I could hardly ask 'Do you mind if we smoke?' with the Prime Minister puffing his head off. So capricious are the impressions we pick up in our way through life that, despite a most memorable visit, if I am ever asked what I thought of 10 Downing Street, I invariably answer: 'They're rather mean with the cigarettes!'

As we were about to leave the PM asked Jim Callaghan if he wanted to come to the door with us. 'I certainly do,' Mr Callaghan had replied, 'It's the only way I'll get my picture in tomorrow's papers!' And he was right. The following morning every paper carried coverage of the visit and most had pictures of the group on the steps of 10 Downing Street.

Four days later Pat, Doris and Arthur hit the picture pages once again, either about to enter the Qantas Boeing 707 Jetliner or happily toasting each other in champagne in the aircraft's first-class lounge. The pictures had been taken the previous day at a specially-arranged 'photo-call' at Heathrow and the papers were dated 17 March the day of departure. After the inevitable Press Conference, a farewell drink at Golden Square and a VIP farewell for ourselves and our families at London Airport the boarding call came and soon we were airborne. If it had not been easy to leave behind the remainder of the cast and the production team to carry on the hard work while we embarked on a pleasure cruise (we thought!) it was much harder to abandon our families. Not because the time apart would be unduly long – we were scheduled to spend three weeks in Australia and two days in San Francisco on the return journey – but because the prospects of the trip were so magical. As it turned out the pressures ahead of us were at times much greater than we would have endured at home but we weren't to know that at the time and there were one or two envious sighs as we left for the departure gate. My wife, as ever, bless her, was philosophical. 'It's just as well I'm not keen on flying,' she said, 'or I *would* feel badly!'

Arthur Leslie was my travelling companion throughout the trip. On the early stages we had taken turns at the window to snap the Alps slipping by under the port wingtip or the lights of Rome as we came in to land. Soon, however, we were seasoned travellers and the cameras were not so busy. There was a lot of time for talk and there could not have been a better companion than Arthur. When he died in 1970 show business lost one of its most talented men and certainly one of its nicest. He was a quiet man who wasn't given to talking about his past but his tremendous value as an actor-manager in the theatre was evidenced by the number of 'big names' who, when visiting Granada, first paid their respects to Arthur. Success had come to him late, almost, he confided, when he thought his career was finished. Finished, although he didn't say it, with little in the way of material reward to show for the years of dedication. And then had come *Coronation Street* and the quiet man who was known only to the repertory audiences of South Lancashire became a national name, a well-known and well-loved face. And he enjoyed every minute of it. I like to think that I was with him at the culmination of that enjoyment. We were cruising in a cloudless sky and the stewardess was setting out the ever-present champagne and savouries when the Captain's voice filled the cabin.

'Hello, ladies and gentlemen! We're flying at forty-two thousand feet and if you'd like to look out of the port windows you'll see we're passing over an island. You may have heard of it. It's Bali.'

There was a moment's silence as Arthur surveyed the glass

of bubbly and, the tray of canapés. 'If anybody had told me ten years ago,' he said, 'that I'd be sitting here drinking champagne and eating caviare forty-two thousand feet over Bali I'd have said he was bloody barmy!' He raised his glass. 'Good health!' he said. It was a toast to a long-awaited and much-deserved reward. But only I knew that. It was the last thing that would have occurred to Arthur.

The red desert of the outback was beneath us and two thousand miles remained to fly when the ladies of the party started to debate what they were going to wear for the arrival in Sydney. Eventually agreement was reached and the ladies disappeared. The transformation from casual travellers to glamorous international stars had begun. Meanwhile Arthur and I discussed the days ahead. 'I know what I'll say when they ask me what I *like* about Australia,' he said, 'but what if they ask me what I *don't* like?' We thought.

'How about cold beer?' I suggested. He liked it.

The thunderclap, twilightless, Australian nightfall had turned out Sydney's lights when the Captain announced our impending arrival at Kingsford Smith Airport. Here was the moment of truth. The historic meeting between *Coronation Street* and a million Aussie fans. The great plane touched down with the same feathery lightness it had displayed at half a dozen airports in the Eastern hemisphere and taxied to a halt. We said goodbye to our third aircrew as the steps were secured and then, suddenly, the doors were open. Holding our collective breaths for the tumult to come we stepped down on to Australian soil. Norman Frisby, our Press Officer, was there to meet us. By himself.

To say that our landing at Sydney was an anti-climax would be a gross understatement. But there were good reasons for the apparent lack of enthusiasm. Our plane was some hours late and those fans who had gathered to greet us had drifted away. More important, we were in the least Anglophile of all Australian cities. Sydney was much nearer to the States, both geographically and culturally, than Melbourne, Adelaide and Perth and local taste ran more to American television than to the products of the Motherland. But what the city lacked in fan-worship it more than made up for in hospitality. Apart from a couple of television interviews and Press conferences our four-day visit was given over to sightseeing and the odd social event, such as an official welcome by the Premier of New South Wales and, the following morning, drinks at the City Hall with the Lord Mayor of Sydney. John Armstrong, Sydney's Lord Mayor, was an engaging character. A Socialist, he found himself in office with a largely Liberal administration but in spite of constant political pressure he maintained a cheerful front. Not only his political enemies were gunning for him, he said. The Press had discovered that a string of sauna baths were being used for purposes not quite as purifying as originally intended and the headlines were stridently reminding him of his promises to 'clean up' the city.

'Did you promise?' we asked him. 'Sure I did!' he said. 'But I meant the litter not the vice!' When, later, Doris Speed, discovering that Australian mayors were professional politicians, asked, 'So you're not in business at all?' the irrepressible Mr Armstrong replied, 'Not originally but now, of course, I'm in the sauna bath business!' Beset on all sides he could still crack a joke.

We had been invited to Australia as guests of the Channel 9 stations which transmitted the *Street* – TCN 9 Sydney, GTV 9 Melbourne and NSW 9 Adelaide. All these stations were part of the giant Packer organization which apparently owned half Australia – the other half being the outback. It wasn't surprising, the Packer influence being what it was, that most doors were open to us. We found ourselves wearing VIP badges at the Royal Sydney Easter Show, presenting the prizes at the National log-chopping competition and being introduced, every five minutes it seemed, to the richest man in Australia. 'Did I say *he* was the richest man in Australia? I'm sorry, he isn't. *This* one is!'

The days were full of sight-seeing. On the obligatory boat-trip round Sydney Harbour, Doris locked herself into the smallest room on the launch and was being rescued by the skipper whilst the rest of us sailed through the shadow of the Harbour Bridge and gawped at the new Opera House. Nor were all our outings organized by our television hosts. Many of Sydney's socialite families wanted to play host to the visiting celebrities and pleasant hours were spent sipping ice-cold drinks by swimming pools, conveniently but safely sited by the shining waters of the harbour. Sharks were often in evidence but if they didn't bother us we certainly didn't bother them.

Whilst the daylight hours were given over largely to Australia's great outdoors, the evenings were taken up by TV chat show appearances, guest spots in TV quiz shows, presenting the annual TV awards and a variety of not-too-arduous social functions. Only our last evening in Sydney was free and that morning I was met by a slightly apprehensive Pat Condon, the TCN 9 producer deputed to look after us. 'I was wondering about a visit to a strip show tonight,' he said. 'Do you think the ladies would object?'

I didn't think so and later in the day he came back to say that he had approached them and they hadn't raised any violent objections. That evening saw us lined up under the catwalk of Sydney's plushiest night-spot. Australian show-biz was by no means as permissive as the Mother Country's at that time and the entertainment was a sort of indoor Bondi Beach with tassels. In spite of this, as one nubile redhead gyrated past us, I caught a disapproving look on Doris's face. 'Hello!' I thought, 'Here it comes!'

She leaned across me. 'Pat!' she said, the disapproval shifting to her voice, 'she should never wear that shade of lipstick with *her* colouring!'

The halcyon days and the velvet nights of Sydney left us totally unprepared for what was to come. The following morning the Ansett-Ana Boeing dropped us into Melbourne Airport and another world. This was hard-core

Coronation Street territory, still British in its tastes and yearning for any link with the Old Country. Here was no Sydney-type anti-climax. Hundreds of fans lined the airport balconies. The Press, too, were waiting for us but they were to be disappointed. We were late arriving and long-standing appointments in the city were already crowding upon us. Cars were waiting, one to whisk me to speak at a lunch-time meeting of the Melbourne Rotary Club, another to take Doris Speed and Arthur Leslie to the GTV 9 studios. Once there, they were rushed through make-up and hurierd in front of a studio audience to tape three programmes of 'Take the Hint', a networked quiz. And that was just the beginning!

Meanwhile I had arrived at an old-fashioned but elegant restaurant at the New Paris end of Melbourne's Collins Street and, after a quick lunch, found myself facing the city's business fraternity barely an hour after touchdown. I usually spoke fairly briefly and then invited questions but first I had to establish a rapport. How was I to do this? How was I to get them on my side? I decided to explore a theory. Were the stories I had heard about inter-state rivalry fact or fiction? Was it true that the antagonism between New South Wales, Victoria and South Australia was so intense that it made Lancashire and Yorkshire look like David and Jonathan? I put it to the test. The previous afternoon, in Sydney, I had trapped my hand rather badly in the door of one of the city's massive American automobiles and my thumb was still heavily bandaged. I lifted it to the waiting audience. 'Forgive the appearance,' I began. 'I was badly bitten in a Sydney nightclub!' The roar of approval answered my unspoken questions. They really did hate the sight of each other! And I was off to a good start.

From that moment we never stopped. We toured, with outrider escort, Melbourne's five Coronation Streets. West Footscray, the city's mainly immigrant suburb, gave us a civic reception. We were received by the Lord Mayor, Ian

Beaurepaire. The artists made personal appearances at the city's stores, presented prizes at a trotting meeting, gave out yet more TV awards, attended Press conferences, it seemed, every couple of hours. Time was found for radio interviews, for writing and taping *Coronation Street* promotions, for appearances on TV interview programmes and on 'In Melbourne Tonight' an open-ended chat show in which Pat, Doris and Arthur performed a sketch I had specially written before leaving England. We toured supermarkets or, at least, those that the huge waiting crowds would let us enter. We attended parties given by the Australian Association of National Advertisers, the British Ex-Servicemen's Legion and the executives of GTV 9. We visited the Children's Hospital and toured the Animal Sanctuary at Healesville. And all this in six days.

Periods of relaxation in Melbourne were few and short-lived and we took full advantage of any break in our commitments. On one occasion, returning from a hectic appearance at a couple of city stores, we came back to our base, the opulent Menzies Hotel, battered and fatigued. Beelines were made for our respective rooms and a well-earned rest before the evening's appointments began but I had no sooner got back to mine than the telephone rang and I was summoned downstairs to talk to a reporter. I found a quiet corner of the lounge and tried desperately to stay awake whilst he plied me with his questions. Whilst this was going on another urgent telephone call came through and Norman Frisby, our Press Officer, began looking for me. He knocked on Arthur Leslie's door. Had he seen me? No, said Arthur, he hadn't. On to Pat Phoenix's room, the same question and the same answer. To Doris Speed and a discreet knock on her door.

'Who is it?' asked Doris through the woodwork.

'It's Norman,' said Norman.

'What on earth do you want?' demanded Doris, weary and none-too-pleased. 'I haven't got a stitch on and I'm just about to get into the shower!'

'Oh, sorry!' said Norman. 'Is Harry with you?'

Light moments were rare in Melbourne though there was exhilaration in plenty. And it wasn't confined to the touring party. *Coronation Street* was breaking down barriers which many Melbourners had thought immovable. Most of the city's newspapers had tie-ups with TV networks. In fact the *Herald*, Melbourne's afternoon paper, owned the rival Channel 7 television station and it was a surprised city which discovered a picture of our arrival on the *Herald*'s front page, the first time that any GTV 9 artists had ever been featured in the paper.

I most enjoyed the quieter hours of the night when Norman Frisby and myself would have a quiet drink and an exchange of views with the executives of GTV. Neither Norman nor I were under the same pressure as the artists and we weren't quite as quick to get to our beds. One discussion, I remember, went on until the early hours. Clyde Packer, at that time supremo of the television side of his father's empire, joined Nigel Dick, the station's managing director, in bemoaning the fact that although Australia could spawn talent it couldn't keep it. I knew this to be true. Shortage of money was still a problem in the Australian industry and they had been unable to woo back the talent they had lost. As I pointed out – and I had only been in the city a few days – the place was teeming with dramatic possibilities. West Footscray, the civic-welcome suburb, was a melting pot not only of differing nationalities but of conflicting emotions. The district was a transit camp, and immigrants who had failed to make good lived cheek by jowl with the hopeful new arrivals, Briton next to Pole, Italian to Yugoslav, some using the area as a springboard to a new life, others as a gloomy staging post on the way back home. Truly a serial writer's paradise. And no one to write it.

Since that night in 1966 the visual arts in Australia have made great strides. Many of the continent's talented sons have returned and an influx of British stars has helped the development of television, stage and large-screen drama. Peter Yeldham, one of the first Australian playwrights to seek fame and fortune in Britain and with whom I worked at Granada in the late fifties, is now back writing scripts for the new wave of Australian cinema. There's plenty of reward for the homecomer. The continent's new polyglot society is far richer in its variety than in Britain. It was both exciting and heartening to see Italians, Greeks and Slavs bringing not only their traditional skills but helping to build the economy in heavier industry, to hear of the Poles moving naturally into the mining areas as, decades earlier, they had populated and enriched North America. But there always has to be a sour note and I found one in Melbourne.

It was on a lunchtime stroll with one of my Channel 9 hosts down the crowded but orderly pavements of Collins Street that I saw something which caused me to turn round and look again. 'What is it?' asked my Australian friend. I told him that I had just seen something for the first time since my arrival in his country – a black face. 'It'll be a student,' he said. I asked him how he could be so sure.

'They're the only black people we allow in,' he said. 'And *he'll* have to leave as soon as he's completed his studies.' It was an unhappy first-hand reminder that, at a time when Britain was beset with immigrant problems, one of the Commonwealth's more civilized members, rich in both space and potential, was failing signally to pull its weight.

On Tuesday, 29 March we left Melbourne for Adelaide. Our arrival at Adelaide Airport was enough to make the entire tour worthwhile. Not only had the waiting fans crowded the balconies of the terminal building but several thousand had overflowed on to the airport apron and our first sight on leaving the plane was of a mass of waving, cheering South Australians held back by barriers and a battery of smiling policemen. Departure through the terminal building was impossible and, formalities forgotten, our cars picked us up on the tarmac and drove us, flanked by police outriders through switched-off traffic lights and a continuous welcoming crowd to the Hotel Australia.

This was the true magic that each of us, secretly, had hoped we might taste. The following day the Press informed us that the reception given to the *Coronation Street* trio was bigger than the Beatles had ever enjoyed and even greater than that given to the Queen Mother who had left the city, comparatively quietly, only the day before. Looking back, it wasn't difficult to understand the warmth generated by the visit of two actresses and an actor from a Lancashire back-street television serial. It wasn't enough to say that South Australia was pro-British. In many respects, the average Adelaider was more 'British' than the British themselves. He was still maintaining standards and moral values which, at home, were in decay. And, as *Coronation Street* had itself avoided the mainstream of permissiveness, the people of Adelaide were, in a strange way, closer to the heart of the programme than was its home audience. At least, that's a theory. Whatever the reason, the people of Adelaide took Pat, Doris and Arthur firmly to their hearts.

Five incredible days followed. A motorcade through the city's streets to a civic reception at the Town Hall led to the breaking, for the first time in the city's history, of Adelaide's Blue Line code. This line, painted down the side of the main roadways had always been accepted by the people as an invisible barrier but the sight of their three idols proved too much. The fans surged forward, breaking the line in their eagerness to shake hands, to touch, to throw gifts, messages and flowers into the open cars. Not that anyone minded. There was a carnival atmosphere in the streets and it was a delight to see so many smiling people. And difficult to suppress a sense of satisfaction in being involved with something which gave so much pleasure to so many so far away from home.

Rob Carless, the Press Officer for NWS 9, the Adelaide station, had carved a middle path between the insouciance of Sydney and the frenzy of Melbourne. The three stars were exhibited but not to extremes; there were personal and TV appearances, but not too many; and everywhere we went, from the Coronation Streets of Adelaide to lunch at Parliament House to a swanky tour of Hardy's Winery in the grape valleys outside the city, we found the same friendliness and nostalgic desire for news of the people and places back home.

We were sorry to leave Adelaide and the farewell they gave us made the parting no easier. The Adelaide *News* estimated that over fifty thousand men, women and children lined the route from our hotel to the airport. Children in pyjamas were snatched from their beds and carried into the streets for a last glimpse and wave; old age pensioners were lifted into wheelchairs and pushed to the nearest vantage point. Everyone, it seemed, wanted to say goodbye.

Two more days in Sydney and it was on, via Fiji and Honolulu, to San Francisco and total anonymity. A young Yellow Cab driver showed us the sights of the city and, on our second day, the redwoods. Inevitably working his way through college and writing a book, he was politely un-impressed when we told him who we were and where we had been. Raised in the land of Columbia and Paramount, stars of show-business were no doubt ten a penny to him. Which was just what we needed. He and his fellow San Franciscans, blissfully unconcerned by their famous visitors, provided the air-lock between the rarefied atmosphere of an ecstatic Australia and the down-to-earth realities of home.

Reunited with our friends and families in London, we returned to Manchester and our last Press Conference on 9 April. It wasn't easy to produce sparkling 'quotes' on demand from the profusion of memories. We had had a wonderful time, we said. The Australian people had been wonderful. The whole trip could only be described as . . . wonderful.

We had been pioneers. American stars aplenty had made the trip to the island continent, performed in its hotel cabarets, waved their ten-gallon hats and departed. We were the first from Britain. Doris Speed, Pat Phoenix and Arthur Leslie, who had gone to represent a modest twice-weekly serial in the southern cities of Australia had become two Britannias and a John Bull, symbols of a life, of cobbled streets and cotton mills, of rain and cloud and hail and snow. Not the most attractive ingredients of nostalgia but none the less yearned for by many an Aussie.

In some ways, looking back, the tour had not been without its elements of cruelty. In spite of the seemingly interminable sunshine, the invigorating air, the golden beaches and the sparkling seas, the hunger for home was barely repressible in many first- and second-generation Australians. Perhaps, in forming a link, in providing so strong a reminder, we had done these people a disservice. I hope not, yet I can still hear the urgency in the voice of the middle-aged woman who grasped Arthur Leslie's arm as we pressed through the crowds in an Adelaide store and implored him, tears running down her face, to 'Take me back home with you!' And she meant every word.

Before the trip started I had harboured two major concerns. The first – how would the Australian people receive us? – had been answered in full. The second, interrelated with the first and the more important of the two – how would our three artists react to the pressures and the adulation they might encounter? I needn't have worried. They gave of themselves unstintingly on what was, despite its glamour, an exhausting and bruising tour. 'Bruising', too, in its literal sense. An Adelaide doctor, treating the trio for swollen hands, informed them that they were suffering from the 'Royal complaint' – caused by the shaking of too many hands. Not only was the tour physically weakening – a clap on the back is a clap on the back however well-meant – it was murder on the ego. The cynic might rightfully argue that the happy-go-lucky Lancashire bonhomie was now second nature to all *Coronation Street* artists but anyone looking down, say, at twenty thousand upturned smiling faces at the new City of Elizabeth and listening to their cheers of welcome could well have been forgiven for becoming a little 'difficult'. But Pat, Doris and Arthur stayed on an even keel. Not only did they carry out a gruelling programme, they each had time for the spontaneous gesture. I remember one morning in Adelaide, standing outside the Hotel Australia waiting with the party to move off on another well-filled day when a thirty-year-old woman pushed her way through the watching fans and nervously approached Pat Phoenix. Her mother, she explained, a great *Street* fan, was bed-ridden and, sorely disappointed at having missed a sight of her favourites, had asked if she might have an autograph.

'Where do you live?' asked Pat. The woman told her. 'Where's that?' Pat asked Rob Carless, our South Australian host. Five minutes away by car, said Rob. 'Come on!' said Pat and the surprised woman found herself being bundled into a limousine and driven home. Not that her surprise was anything to her mother's when, sitting up in bed she watched as the door opened and a glamorous, smiling Elsie Tanner popped her head round, said 'Hello, love! They tell me you're poorly!' and stayed for a chat and a cup of tea.

The secret of the tour's success was perhaps best summed up by a sardonic member of the Australian Press corps. We had been warned that the Aussie journalist was the most murderous of the breed but the trip was going so well that we took our courage in both hands and agreed to a full-scale Press reception. The junket was held at the Great Eastern Hotel at Littlehampton in the hills above Adelaide and, after a wary start, artists, assassins and associates began to enjoy the boar's heads and barons of beef, the Foster's lager and the native (and excellent) champagne. At two o'clock in the morning I was buttonholed by a gaunt Pressman who pressed a glass of something-or-other in my hand and plied me with a few searching questions. Then he paused and looked at me.

'I'll tell you something!' he said. 'When we heard that

you Poms were coming over we got out the knives and we sharpened them good. We were really going to carve you up!' His eyes flickered to Pat and Doris, fresh as the morning dew, Pat regaling one group with some tale of home, Doris holding court with another. And, between them, Arthur Leslie demonstrating to a bleary band of reporters the gentle art of opening a champagne bottle. 'But these bastards . . .!' the Pressman went on, his voice full of wonder, '. . . these bastards'd charm the birds from the bleedin' trees!'

CHAPTER TEN

'If I'm payin' the piper, I'm callin' the tune!'

Len Fairclough

Mention has been made earlier in these pages of the latent power of *Coronation Street*. When one considers that, in its heyday, the serial was seen twice a week by well over half the population of the British Isles, it is not surprising that it was viewed with some envy as an instrument of both advertisement and propaganda. During my ten years as producer I was constantly being reminded – no doubt in the hope of some revolutionary quote – that with *Coronation Street*'s power over the people I could quite easily bring down the Government. My stock reply – as mild-mannered as I could manage – was that that was not my brief. My brief was to entertain and although it might be argued that the bringing down of some Governments of either colour could fairly be described as superb entertainment, that wasn't how I saw my job.

The smaller pressures were more difficult to resist. Often, in pubs, I would have a large whisky pressed into my hand and an unknown face would smile at me and a strange voice call me by my Christian name and ask how I would like a wonderful new cigarette display on the counter of the Rovers Return. These requests invariably met with a cool response but that didn't stop them coming. Had we given in to these inducements the show would have been swamped with outside influences just as present-day professional sport is in danger of being swamped.

Television's attitude to sponsorship has blown hot and cold over the years. As the American example has tended to show, in any sponsored programme, given a straight fight

131

between artistic and commercial values, money will always win. It follows then that the programme must lose some of its integrity and this sadly also applies when a show allows itself to be used for propaganda purposes, however much this may appear to be in the national interest. *The Archers* is an unhappy example. Involved as I am in the serial world, I am always interested in other examples of the art form and at one time I was a regular listener to the BBC's tale of country folk. My interest, however, began to wane when it seemed that the producers of the programme allowed themselves to be persuaded by some astute Government PRO that they had a great power for good. One began almost to hear the footsteps of the young messenger boy as he raced down the corridors of the BBC carrying the latest message from the Ministry of Agriculture and Fisheries for inclusion in that night's episode.

'Arggh!' Dan Archer would say. 'They've had another outbreak of foot and mouth down Hereford way!' and the heavy breathing in the background was not the reaction of his listeners but the messenger boy trying to get his puff back. It can and will be argued that these inclusions were real, that farming folk do speak of such things but, just as the shaggy dog was 'too damned shaggy' so, in a drama programme, such realities are 'too damned real'. The public are pretty astute at picking out these points and by and large they object to their favourite programmes being used for the dissemination of official information.

Coronation Street, being a television programme, had the edge over *The Archers*. It could help not only verbally but visually and it was not surprising that the Decimalization Board sought our help in familiarizing the British public with that strange new coin, the fifty pence piece, when it first came into circulation. I was approached by the Board some months before this coin burst upon a suspicious public. On this occasion no story, as such, was needed. The coin, when it became legal tender on 15 October of decimilization year, would become part of British life and would be passed backwards and forwards across the counters of our corner shop and the Rovers Return. I agreed to help and pointed out that as we recorded some weeks before transmission I would need the coin, for use as a 'prop', well in advance of the issue date.

Whilst I was waiting for the coin to arrive I mentioned the exercise to one of the chaps in Granada's Sales Department and asked him what the coverage which *Coronation Street* would be able to give would have cost the Decimalization Board had they been forced into the normal advertising channels. He hazarded a guess at thirty thousand pounds. A couple of days later the newly-minted coin arrived together with a letter of thanks from the Decimalization Board for any help I would be able to give and asking me to return the coin after use. Thirty thousand pounds worth of free publicity and they wanted their fifty pence back! On Monday, 15 October, *Coronation Street*'s audience saw Len Fairclough push the fifty pence piece across the bar of the Rovers Return to Jack Walker.

Jack pushed it back. 'I don't want any of your foreign rubbish in here,' he said.

Len pushed it back again. 'That's not foreign rubbish,' he said, 'that's British rubbish.'

I learned later that I had perhaps been unduly harsh in my assessment of the Decimalization Board as the meanest moguls of Whitehall. The Treasury, I found, was forbidden by law from giving money away.

Not every Government department asked for our help. Some criticized us, always vociferously, often unfairly. There was a body of opinion in Britain that *Coronation Street* was projecting a bad image of the North-West of England. Not surprisingly this was seized upon by the Press and culminated in a telephone call which woke me up in the middle of one night. The television reporter of a national daily newspaper, browsing through his Press Association reports, had come across one which quoted from a speech made by a high-up in the Ministry of Regional Development the previous evening. *Coronation Street*, the Junior Minister had thundered, was not only a travesty of the truth but was dealing a death blow at the nation's economy. Young executives, dismayed by the picture the serial painted of the North-West of England, had refused to move there from their native South, with the result that an imbalance of management had been created, the region's capabilities were seriously affected and disaster loomed ahead.

The television reporter asked me if I had any comment. 'At three o'clock in the morning,' I told him, 'you bet I have a comment. You can tell the Junior Minister and any-one else who's interested that if these young executives honestly believe that the North of England is one huge cobbled street covered with terraced houses and have never heard of the Peak District, Lakeland, the Lancashire Fells and the green and fertile plains of Cheshire then they are very under-educated young executives indeed and we'd rather they stayed where they were.'

Granada has always been a politically-conscious company. Trend-setters in political television, they challenged the view that television reporting of elections was illegal by covering the Rochdale by-election in February 1958. Nor was this penchant confined to the screen. In the late fifties and early sixties, political soirées were regular events at Granada's Manchester studios. Members of Parliament representing the constituencies in Granadaland were in-vited for a bun, a drink and a chat with Granada's producers, administrators and executives, and exhausting affairs they were for anyone not steeped in matters politic.

On one of these occasions, having escaped from a suc-cession of fervent young MPs and their blue-stocking wives, all of whom steadfastly believed (and not without reason) that their pet subject would better catch the public ear coming from the bar of the Rovers Return than from the back benches of the House of Commons, I found myself being introduced to Harold Wilson's father. Mr Wilson senior, whose personal political ambitions had led him no further than Huddersfield's mayoral parlour, had far greater aspirations for his heir and it was fascinating to see how the old man's eyes rarely left his son's figure. After five minutes conversation it was easy to see that Harold Wilson's journey to the upper echelons of the Labour Party had not been without the utmost in parental push and prayer.

Later that same evening I was introduced to Harold Wilson himself. At that time he was Shadow Chancellor under Gaitskell's leadership. In a way we were both professional Northerners and the talk soon turned to matters Northern in general and *Coronation Street* in particular. Mr Wilson had many complimentary things to say about the programme but he was worried that its virtues were not so readily accepted by his Southern colleagues. He quoted an example. Gaitskell, he said, had suggested a meeting of the Shadow Cabinet and had put forward a Wednesday evening as a suitable date and when Mr Wilson had demurred, saying that Mondays and Wednesdays were his *Coronation Street* nights, his leader had been amazed! And so was I! Were meetings of Her Majesty's Shadow Cabinet really postponed so that one of its more important members could watch a half-hour episode of a twice-weekly television serial? Or did Mr Wilson genuinely believe that I would happily accept his fable as some sort of compliment?

Television's twin potential parasitical elements – Government and sponsorship – are mercifully absent to any dangerous degree from the British medium. It would however be unwise to be too complacent about either. Although successive Governments have studiously avoided any suggestion of control it must be remembered that television has only been the powerful force it is for a relatively short time. Governments tend to curb any outside power when they feel themselves under threat and this, as far as television is concerned, has so far not happened. Which

135

is not to say that it will not happen at some future date. Freedom of speech is one thing when given to the individual whose voice carries only a few yards, quite another when applied to a force which controls the news and views brought into ninety-five per cent of British homes. The prophecies of '1984' may be a little premature but it will be interesting to see what the year 2000 brings. The Labour Party's complaints about the right-wing Press, some of them justified, give a foretaste of what might happen were television to swing violently in any political direction. One thing is sure. If the medium does fall under Governmental control, the State and television will be equally to blame.

Sponsorship, the more insidious of the two parasites, is already a part of British life. As a boy, watching Bradman carve out his double centuries at Manchester's Old Trafford Ground, I never envisaged the day when no Test match could be played without the financial support of some insurance company or other. It was inconceivable, seeing Finney and Matthews weave their magic on the wings, that their 1981 counterparts would be plastered in advertising material. No professional sport appears to have escaped the attentions of the advertising sponsor, some of them quite intriguing. What discussions, for example, led to the array of Robinson's bottles behind the player's head as he takes his seat by the umpire's chair at Wimbledon? And invariably with every label turned firmly towards the camera! It would, however, be a spoilsport, in every sense of the word, who condemned such practices out of hand. In the areas of big spending, big money is always welcome and as long as these infusions of advertising cash do not destroy the sports themselves then they could be said to be preserving something which, without them, might die.

Television sponsorship, however, conceals more subtle dangers. Whilst there is no recorded instance of any sponsor telling Kevin Keegan how to play his game or Geoffrey Boycott how to execute a cover drive, in television it is a short step from controlling the money supply to controlling the programme content. That a programme like *Death of a Princess* might seriously damage the foreign policy of Her Majesty's Government can never be more than cause for regret, but Heaven help the sponsored producer who tries to put anything into his programme which might harm the product. And this is by no means the only constriction under which such producers must operate. In New York the lunch-time soap operas make impossible demands on their production teams. The sponsors appear to be concerned only with the length of screen time in which they can air their product. It is not unusual for an American soap opera to run for fifty minutes every weekday and when one realizes that *Coronation Street* has the greatest difficulty in producing an acceptable fifty minutes each *week* it will be seen that these demands cannot be other than destructive. Rehearsal time on such shows can be as short as a single morning for each fifty-minute episode and it is hardly surprising that the finished product bears little relation to a script which has been put together with a great deal of professional expertise. It must be heartbreaking for such producers and writers to see their talents wasted in such a manner. No doubt they just take the money and run.

Happily sponsorship of this type has not yet reached Britain and one can only hope it never will. But whilst the millions of pounds worth of advertising money may not yet control the content of our programmes, they can and do affect, in some small ways, their production. As long ago as 1964, when I was producing *The Villains* for Granada, a part cropped up that was ready-made for Betty Driver, now, I am pleased to say, a *Coronation Street* regular but at that time better known as 'Mum' in a famous soap powder commercial. The part I wanted her for was motherly, too, with the slight difference that our character was the wife of a petty criminal who made delicate sandwiches and copious pots of tea for her husband and his comic confederates when they met to discuss the next job. Betty's agent asked to see the script which was duly passed on to the advertising agency and ultimately we were regretfully informed that Betty could not be released from her contract as the part would damage her soap powder image!

In many ways the BBC is far more lax in its attitude to in-programme advertising than are the independent companies, a supposition which gains strength when one realizes that ITV's attitude is governed by law and the BBC's by a code of practice. However, apart from the odd monumental lapse both networks show a sensible regard for sponsorship and a healthy suspicion of its consequences. Long may it remain so.

CHAPTER ELEVEN

'I can manage numbers – it's figures I'm no good at!'

Bet Lynch

There are, some people would have us believe, lies, damned lies and statistics yet every day sane men and women risk their futures and their fortunes on the product of some poll or other. At the other end of the spectrum politicians bend these figures to their advantage. To watch a Tory, a Socialist and a Liberal discussing on TV the results of the latest by-election is to watch verbal and numerate conjuring at its very best.

Where lies the truth? Are statistics all things to all men or are they clear, unequivocal illustrations of the truth? I know that where television ratings are concerned I base my answer on a simple premise. Asked if I believe the JICTAR (Joint Industry Committe for Television Advertising Research) ratings I will say 'yes'. Asked why, I will explain that if hard-headed, money-conscious advertisers trust them in planning their various campaigns (and in spending millions of pounds each year) then I will trust them too. Money talks and one of the things it says is 'I believe'.

The measurement of a television audience has always been a suspect enterprise. The man in the street, I find, tends not to believe the claims of BBC and ITV, particularly when, at times such as Christmas, they tend to differ alarmingly. However, I think he is wrong to be so incredulous. The differing figures (and usually the difference is slight) are due to differing methodologies – the BBC prefers the human touch, researchers, street questionnaires and the like; JICTAR goes further and fixes meters to a representative number of TV sets, their findings supplementing the data provided by a diary kept by each mature member of each chosen household. Believe what you will. Personally I have always harboured a niggling suspicion that the only way to get away from a BBC street researcher if one is in a hurry is to say that one watched BBC-1 for the entire previous evening and enjoyed every minute of it!

Conflicting audience figures may soon be a thing of the past. Talks are under way between the various interested bodies – BBC, independent companies, advertisers and statisticians – which will, I hope, lead to the introduction of a single system of television audience measurement. It could be that by the end of 1981 only one service will be in operation, meeting the needs of all the interested parties.

Misguided cynicism is not restricted to the measurement of audiences. A great deal of hot air is let off about how those audiences are obtained. The Press (which dislikes television on two counts – first that TV 'prints' the news before they can, and second that commercial television pinched some of its advertising revenue) is always quick to talk of 'the ratings war' and to condemn companies and producers for the methods they employ in winning an audience. What, I would ask, do they expect us to do? Would they condemn a theatre owner for wanting to sell every seat? A football club for wanting to fill the terraces? A newspaper for wanting a huge readership?

Show me a television producer who doesn't care whether or not he gets an audience for his productions and I'll show you a man who doesn't deserve to be in the business. The medium is too important to offer sanctuary to the self-indulgent, and whatever the producer's role – to entertain, to inform or to educate – he must try his damnedest to attract as big an audience as he can. Which isn't to say there is no room for programmes of minority interest but *is* to say that the producer's job is to expand that interest. Given the Albert Hall for the meeting of some obscure movement the aim should not be to huddle in a corner but to quicken popular curiosity so that every seat is filled.

Much has been said and written about competition between the BBC and Independent Television. More often than not this results in the viewer having to miss a programme he would normally wish to see although, with the advent and growing popularity of the video cassette recorder this is becoming less of a problem. In the past, however, this apparent lack of concern for the public excited angry comment. 'Why can't they get together?' rose the cry. And do what? Agree not to interfere with known favourites on the other channel? Ask a producer to create a half hour that no one will want to watch in order to allow a clear field for the favourite show on the 'other side'? The truth is that competition is an accepted ingredient in the process of improvement in every field. Why should television be so different? Do newspapers defer to each other? Theatre managers tell the public to see the show next door? Far from it, they compete fiercely and it is not wrong for television to follow suit.

In the early years of *Coronation Street* it appeared that the BBC had no heart for a fight. This, coupled with the Equity strike of 1961/2 which, whilst crippling most ITV shows, allowed *Coronation Street* to stagger on with a contracted cast of thirteen, were potent factors in the programme's meteoric rise to the top of the Top Ten. It wasn't until the arrival of Bryan Cowgill to the Controllership of BBC-1 that the *Street* found itself with a battle on its hands. Mr Cowgill, straight from a job as BBC's Head of Sport, was obviously spoiling for a fight and suddenly we found ourselves with first runs of *Till Death Us Do Part* and *Steptoe and Son*, firm favourites of the day and strong opposition to even the most entrenched programme. The result was immediate. *Coronation Street* slipped several places down the ratings and any complacency there may have been was hurriedly thrown out of the window. It is interesting to listen to Bryan Cowgill on the subject:

In planning a programme schedule to compete with any guarantee of success against *Coronation Street*, I had to accept in the first instance that I was up against that most formidable of all popular entertainments on television – a favourite programme that has become an institution. It seemed to me the only hope was to avoid at all costs a head-to-head confrontation beginning at 7.30 pm. The best chance, I felt, was to straddle that particular junction with a programme or combination of programmes designed as far as possible to entertain a vast audience with a mix of hit comedy and drama which would distract from *Coronation Street*'s starting time of 7.30 pm. On occasion it worked, but you really can't keep a good institution down unless you are lucky enough to develop something equally formidable. In the case of *Coronation Street* the simple fact of competitive television scheduling is that nothing has come along so far to claim a stronger hold, year in and year out, on the heart as well as the interest of that huge audience settling down for the evening in front of the television set. As every experienced television programmer knows, the techniques of popular scheduling search always for the programme which will consistently entertain the nation in the early part of an evening and hand on a significant number to the programmes that follow. Apart from its other merits, *Coronation Street* remains the longest established record-holder in these particular stakes – and the stakes are extremely high.

Bryan Cowgill is not alone in his beliefs. No less authoritative a publication than the *Encyclopaedia Britannica* takes a similar view. Their contributor on world television writes:

Some of the characters in radio and television serials develop with time, living almost natural life-spans over the years and becoming familiar to a public numbered in millions. An outstanding example is the British television serial *Coronation Street*, which by 1971 had been playing twice weekly for ten years to an average audience large enough to keep a theatre filled for 130 years. To many of its followers, the characters in *Coronation Street* are as real as their friends next door.

(From 'Television and Radio, Arts of' in *Encyclopaedia Britannica*, 15th edition (1974), 18:125.)

When Bryan Cowgill brought a competitive edge to BBC-1 he started a process which continues unabated today. Many popular drama series find themselves pitted against the *Street* with varying degrees of success. In 1980 a re-run of *Dallas* on BBC-2 from the beginning to the famous 'Who shot J.R.?' episode failed to dent *Coronation Street*'s ratings. Which, in view of the BBC's sometimes frantic publicity campaign in support of its American import, is surprising. The truth is, of course, that nowadays the BBC is much more of a commercial channel than is ITV.

There is no doubt that the BBC's publicity department has a loud voice in the corridors of power whereas ITV's fragmented promotion machine is rather muted.

I recall writing a memo of complaint to my Granada superiors on this very subject. At the end of each year the *Daily Telegraph* used to commission a Gallup Poll to ask its readers various questions on popular entertainment. One of the questions was: 'What in your opinion was the best television programme of [in this case] 1970?' The answer was 1. *Coronation Street*, 2. *Family at War*. The BBC had a little earlier embarked on a eulogistic publicity exercise over their award-winning programmes and I could not see why we should not do something similar to advertise our *Daily Telegraph* success, particularly as the result indicated a strong middle-class following for our programme. The result was disappointing. A press release was issued on the subject which, in view of the *Telegraph*'s involvement, was ignored by the rest of Fleet Street. I cannot believe that 'Auntie BBC' would have been guilty of such mute acceptance of public acclaim, but when I pointed this out to my bosses I was reminded that *Coronation Street* was already seen by half Britain's viewing population so what more did I want? To which I could only reply – 'the other half'.

Whilst on the subject of recognition, it is interesting to note that *Coronation Street* has always been acknowledged more materially by the viewing public than by the profession itself. Over the years, the readers of many popular newspapers besides the *Daily Telegraph*, from the *Sun* and the *Daily Mirror* in Britain to the New Zealand *Herald*, have voted the serial their number one favourite and its artists have headed many a popularity poll. Professional bodies inside the television industry have, however, been cooler, preferring the 'starburst' programme, which more briefly illuminates the firmament, to the 'bread and butter' shows which form the viewer's staple diet. However, in recent times, both the Writers' Guild of Great Britain and BAFTA (British Academy of Film and Televisual Arts) have given special awards to the serial whilst, in the middle ground, the Silver Hearts of the Variety Club have found their way to *Coronation Street*. But, pleasant though it is to gather them, given the choice between trophies and a large, loyal audience I would always plump for the latter.

This desire for the mass audience has never, I hope, manifested itself in gimmickry. In a serial such as the *Street* which deals with largely mundane subjects it is difficult (even if it were wanted) to contrive sensational cliffhangers of, say, the *Dallas* type. Birth, marriage and death are still our top three topics with money a close fourth, and these crop up with natural regularity. There are rare occasions, however, where a specific attempt can be made to increase the size of the audience and where success in doing so can actually be measured. So rare are these that I can only remember one. In late September 1962 we were planning the story of the 'snatching of Christopher, two-month-old son of Harry and Concepta Hewitt. John Finch was to write that particular sequence and the decision we had to make was whether or not to show the baby alive and well at the end of the episode in which the kidnapping had taken place. In the original script Finch had us see the baby gurgling happily in the arms of his abductress but I argued that to leave the viewers in suspense would be to guarantee a sizeable audience for the following Monday's episode. We discussed the pros and cons. Would it be too harrowing to leave twenty million viewers for five days not knowing whether the baby was dead or alive? Would it be unwise to 'blow' the story too soon and deny our loyal followers the opportunity to work out the outcome for themselves?

In the end I decided to take out the final scene and see what happened. It was soon obvious that, in terms of interest creation, the move had been sound. The fate of Baby Christopher became the major talking points in shops, factories and on the streets of Britain throughout the next few days and it was clear that the following Monday night audience would be a big one. Just how big we didn't realize at the time. On the Friday of the week following the transmission of that episode I was in my office when a messenger brought in the TAM (Tabulated Audience Measurement) Top Twenty sheet for the previous week. Not only was *Coronation Street* in first and second positions but a footnote proclaimed that the Monday audience was the highest recorded in the history of British television. The programme's lead over its nearest rival that week amounted to more than 1.5 million homes or almost 4 million viewers. The full Top Twenty and the Regional Top Tens are reprinted in the illustrations section. The JICTAR ratings for the week ending 29 June 1980 can also be seen there. Once again *Coronation Street* holds the top two positions and once again its lead over the third most popular programme is considerable. And these two sets of figures are almost eighteen years apart!

As Bryan Cowgill pointed out, the role of the early evening programme is not only to win viewers for itself but to build a substantial audience which will remain tuned to that channel for the rest of the night's viewing. This is becoming more difficult as viewers become more sophisticated and selective. No longer are tuner knobs rusted to ITV, as the BBC have proved in their successful assaults on the ratings. However, the fact remains that programmes following the top shows 'inherit' sizeable audiences, and whenever I was producing or writing outside the *Street* I was never averse to my new show appearing on a Monday or a Wednesday evening. And preferably at eight o'clock on either! Much has been made of the BBC Saturday night stranglehold on the mass audience. This is largely due to strong, popular programmes in the early evening. By the time ITV screens its blockbuster film or its star-studded variety show the British audience is comfortably settled – and watching the other side.

The question is often asked: 'Do ratings matter?' and when one considers some of the multi-million-pound projects which have been watched by three men and a dog it is easy to understand these doubts. An expensive production's failure to figure in the Top Twenty does not necessarily condemn it for ever. It may be a co-production – a joint exercise with some overseas television service – and the costs may be recouped and the popularity enjoyed in that other country. It may be a prestige production and every network must be forgiven for sliding a few of these into its schedules, as long as it doesn't do so to the detriment of the rest of its output. This, however, is the Beluga caviare side of television. When one asks whether the ratings of bread and butter programmes such as *Coronation Street* matter, the answer must be an unqualified 'yes'.

The path of television audience preference is easily charted. Up to the mid-fifties the BBC, unchallenged, maintained a somewhat disdainful monopoly. The shadow of Reith still hung over the Corporation and the evening-suited news-readers and the upper middle-class attitudes of most of its programmes belonged to a world far removed from that of the bulk of its growing audience. There was little doubt that, given a choice, many viewers would switch to ITV and its rich aroma of showbiz and this is precisely what happened. For many years the independent networks ruled the roost but a combination of events brought back a healthy competitive element to British television. Firstly, the ITA (later to become the IBA with the advent of commercial radio), somewhat ashamed of the brashness of its charges, called a halt to the super-popular give-away quiz programmes which filled the schedules in the late fifties and sixties. Secondly, and by far the more important, the BBC's men at the top decided to fight. It must be remembered that by the middle sixties there had been an interchange of personnel not only from the BBC to the new independent network but back again to the BBC. And those who went back took with them some of the buccaneering spirit of the new network. By the seventies battle was well and truly joined and no longer can it be said that either side holds a monopoly. It is true that in certain areas of programming one side or the other holds an advantage. It is generally conceded, for instance, that the BBC is superior in the fields of situation comedy and the classic serial, although some forays into these areas by the independents have proved very successful. Similarly the BBC has not yet been able to match Granada and Yorkshire TV in their two twice-weekly serials, although there must be sufficient people on the production side of the BBC who are eminently capable of mounting a worthy challenger. It is almost as though both sides have ceded territory to each other which they have promised not to invade.

A quick glance at the two Top Twenty ratings reproduced in the illustrations section will reveal what appears at first sight to be a puzzle. In the list of October 1962, *Coronation Street*, at No. 1, was viewed in 8,868,000 homes, a total audience of well over 20,000,000. By June 1980 this top audience had shrunk to 14,650,000 viewers and yet it is a fact that during the intervening eighteen years many, many homes installed their first television set. Even allowing for seasonal viewing habits this merits investigation. The answer lies in the growing attraction of a largely unsung newcomer to the scene – BBC-2. This network, originally the Third Programme of television, now contains a successful blend of repeats, arts programmes and popular inventions of its own. There is little doubt that, although BBC-2 shows do not as yet figure in the Top Twenty, the network is now making a considerable impact on the nation's viewing habits.

Whatever the economic and political factors behind 'the ratings war' may be, the simple truth remains that what keeps the battle at fever pitch is no more and no less than the personal pride of the combatants. Everyone dreams of riding the winner of the Derby, captaining a victorious Test side, scoring the winning goal at Wembley or, if you produce a television programme, guiding it to the top of the heap. And as things stand there's only one yardstick which tells you when you're there. No use going to your friends – they tell you a load of rubbish. Certainly no use going to your employers – they'd be frightened of praising you in case you asked for an increase in salary. No, the only yardstick is the JICTAR ratings. Admittedly they don't tell you which is the 'best' programme (whatever that may mean) but they do indicate which shows have the power to attract and, in the case of the long-running programme, those which pull in and keep a huge, loyal, obviously entertained audience week after week. And no programme has given its producers more Derby winners, more victorious sides to captain, more winning goals than *Coronation Street*.

CHAPTER TWELVE

'I bought an exercise book and I wrote this lovely play
in my best handwriting and I sent it to the BBC. They
sent it back by t'next post. I'm sure nobody had read it.'

Hilda Ogden

There is a popular fallacy – which has been going the
rounds for the past twenty years – that the cast of *Coronation
Street* walk into the studio at 7.30 on Mondays and Wednesdays, stand in front of the cameras and make it up as they
go along. I continue to be a great admirer of actors and
their abilities but having been subjected to the less than
deathless prose some of them come out with when asked to
ad lib, this, looking at it one way, can hardly be seen as a
compliment to those who actually write the programmes.
However I hopefully suspect that a compliment *is* intended
and that those who support the fallacy do so because they
consider the dialogue too lifelike to have been manu-
factured.

The truth is that *Coronation Street* is very heavily scripted
indeed. Given the fact that the programme must produce
two twenty-five minute episodes between Monday and
Friday of each week of the year, the more help the script
can give to cast, director and designer the better. The two
scripts reach the chosen director only two weeks before his
week of production and during that period he must plan
his studio lay-out with his designer, decide his rehearsal
schedule, calculate his wardrobe, 'prop' and make-up
needs, cast any new characters and work out his dramatic
and technical approach to the episodes, that is to say, how
he will 'pace' the various scenes emotionally and how he will
arrange his cameras and sound booms to produce the best

story-telling pictures. When one considers that, for the average fifty-minute play, a director is allowed up to six weeks' preparation, it will be appreciated that the fortnight given to the *Street* director allows little time for long and abstruse debate on the meaning of the written word. Which explains why the question 'What exactly do you *mean* by this scene?' whilst often asked in the other corridors of television is rarely heard in *Coronation Street*. By the time a *Street* script reaches the director it is expected to be oven-ready.

Coronation Street's scripting procedure has been explained in an earlier chapter. Each writer is given a synopsis, a scene-by-scene breakdown not only of the episode he has been commissioned to write but of all other episodes so that he has available to him the lead-up to and the development of his stories, helpful information in planning his own script. This synopsis is called a storyline and is intended, not as gospel, but as a guide to the writer. He can if he wishes alter the order of scenes, put available characters into scenes in the script in which they do not appear in the storyline and introduce inconsequential subjects of his own so long as, at the end of the day, he has used only the settings and characters given to him and has told the stories given by the storyline, no more and no less. This latter point is most important. If a writer, given stages one, two and three of a story to develop, fails to cover stage three then there will be a puzzling gap in continuity; if he goes on to develop stages four and five (which belong to the next script) there will be repetition. And by repetition I don't mean 'recapping'. It is a mortal sin to play the same scene twice but quite forgivable – even necessary – to remind viewers of past happenings by discussing them in the following episode, usually between different characters than those at first involved.

Having read and re-read his synopsis and decided what alterations, if any, he wants to make, the writer puts the first piece of paper into the typewriter (or takes up his pen if he's a longhand merchant) lifts his eyes to Heaven and starts to think. The first two words are easy – SCENE ONE – what follows is more difficult. His first job is to set the scene for the opening piece of action – whether film or studio, when and where it takes place, what characters are present, where they stand or sit in relation to each other. He must also briefly describe any new characters as and when they enter the scene. He may even go so far as to indicate with which particular 'shot' he wishes the director to open the scene though there is no guarantee that the director will agree with him over this. For instance:

SCENE 5. STUDIO. OGDENS' LIVING-ROOM I PM
Open on Eddie struggling to get a largish Christmas tree through the door. Stan and Hilda watch from inside the room. Hilda frowns at the falling needles.

. . . or

SCENE 13. FILM. THE STREET. 2.45 PM
A high shot from the factory. One or two pedestrians. A woman turns the Rovers corner into the street. She checks the house numbers, walks up to the Ogdens'. As she knocks cut to a close shot. This is Mrs Palin. She's in her mid-thirties, fadedly pretty, neatly but poorly dressed. She has obviously made an effort. She looks, rather puzzled, at the shabby house. Hilda opens the door.

Although these examples may appear on the sketchy side, some writers give even less information in their stage directions. Some merely give the place and time, dive straight into the dialogue and let the director get on with it but I have always believed that although it is the director's prerogative to use or discard the information given, the writer has had the decided advantage of seeing the action in his mind's eye when he wrote the episode and it would be quite wrong of him to keep what he saw to himself. But not all writers 'see' what they write. Those who, like the radio writer, merely hear the action and concentrate all their efforts on the dialogue, need the 'eye' of the director to help produce the finished article.

Listening to the dialogue as you write it is no less important than seeing the action. Only by listening does the writer realize that certain speeches may be misinterpreted and spoken in the wrong way. It is then that he uses 'speech directions' – indications to the actor as to how a particular line should be delivered. Some actors consider these to be faintly insulting but even the best of them can make mistakes and it is better to be sure than sorry. For instance:

STAN

(*A whine*) I can't clean winders with a heavy frost, can I?

HILDA

(*Aggressive*) You can with a shammy leather but not from where you're sitting!

Although Jean Alexander and Bernard Youens, who play Hilda and Stan are totally in control of their characters, the two directions used in this example save any possible argument at rehearsal as to who should be the dominant partner in the exchange. Without the directions Stan could deliver his line forcefully and Hilda say hers apologetically.

Stage directions do more than describe movement and action. To me they complete the story, and make the script a readable piece in its own right. It has long been my philosophy that work should be as enjoyable as one can possibly make it and to this end I try to heighten the tension or continue the comedy inside the stage directions themselves. These efforts never reach the viewer but I think they remind the actor that making television drama is not all blood, toil, sweat and tears and if you can have a bit of fun while you're doing it this tends to shine through.

Coronation Street's great gift to its writers is its infinite variety. Inside one script (Episode 2056, transmitted on 15 December 1980) I was asked to write comedy scenes between the Ogdens and Eddie Yeats, their dustbinman lodger; tragic conversations between Emily Swain and Flora Swain, wife and sister of Arnold Swain recently unmasked as a bigamist; domestic exchanges between Ivy and Bert Tilsley, at that time sampling the doldrums of unemployment; and inconsequential chat scenes in the Rovers about anything that came to mind. This is how they appear on the written page:

SCENE I. STUDIO. OGDENS' LIVING-ROOM 10 AM

Stan at the table, the racing page spread before him. He is writing his selections on a pad before him. Hilda enters, pooped from a stint at the Rovers. She sits facing him, looks at him distastefully. He glances up, nods briefly and goes back to his paper. Eventually . . .

HILDA

(*Dangerously quiet*) Know what *I* fancy?

STAN

What?

HILDA

The cup that cheers.

STAN

(*Checking the paper*) It's not runnin'.

HILDA

(*Flaring*) No and neither are you, you big lummox! Get off your fat bottom and get me one!

STAN

(*Aggrieved*) I've only just this minute sat down!

HILDA

Because you've only just this minute got up! I've been out since eight o'clock, workin' me fingers to the bone, Lady Muck standin' over me makin' sarky remarks and for why? I'll tell you for why. To bring money into this house, to buy food to make you fatter and flamin' lazier that's for why! Well I'll tell you Stanley, I've had enough!

153

Things are going to change! And fast! For a start, how much were you going to put on them four-legged money-eaters?

STAN

Only a quid!

HILDA

Put it on the table!

STAN

(*A whine*) I feel lucky!

HILDA

You *are* lucky! I've kept my hands off you! The pound note – put it on the table! (*Reluctantly Stan does as he's told. Hilda picks it up*) Right, that can go to a worthier cause for a start! Get in that kitchen and brew a fresh pot o' tea.

STAN

You don't half lead me a flamin' dog's life!

HILDA

A what? Stop fancyin' yourself! You'd come in last at flamin' Crufts! (*This is unfair. He's looking like a pedigree spaniel*) Go on! *He levers himself out of the chair and chunners his way to the kitchen. The front door opens and closes and Eddie enters, rubbing his hands together.*

EDDIE

By the left, it's parky out there!

HILDA

(*Shouting*) Put an extra teabag in. Eddie wants a cup!

EDDIE

Oh, very kind! Got Stanley doin' his whack, have you? (*Hilda flashes him a look*) Under the whip, is he?
Stan enters, picks up the teapot.

STAN

All right for you two to sit down, isn't it?

EDDIE

You cheeky devil! I've just done four an' a half hours
solid graftin'. Me fingers were freezin' to the bin handles!

HILDA

(*To Stan*) An' seein' you brought the subject up, why are
you sittin' down instead of up a ladder?

STAN

I can't clean winders in *this* weather! (*Eddie and Hilda
look at each other*) Ask any pro winder cleaner! We work
twice as hard in summer to make up. (*Hilda and Eddie
look at each other again*)

HILDA

Twice as hard as what?

STAN

(*Weakly*) You know! *Twice* as hard!

HILDA

Didn't it occur to you, Stanley, just for one split second of
that idle life of yours, didn't it occur to you that there
might be one or two jobs needed doin' round the house?
Like puttin' the Christmas decorations up for a start.

EDDIE

Why not? Let a little festive colour into us dull lives!

STAN

What's the point? You've only got to take 'em down
again.

HILDA

(*To Eddie*) Why do we get up in the mornin', we only go
back to bed?

EDDIE

He's been askin' himself that question for years, haven't
you, Stanley?

Could *I* ask a question? When are we gettin' that flamin' tea?

I . . . er . . . I don't think I switched the kettle on!

You . . . ! (*She takes a swing at him, connects*)

At this point the storyline cuts to a scene in the corner shop between Alf Roberts and Len Fairclough. The story-line makes no reference to the preceding scene but, by 'seeing' the pictures and knowing that the Ogdens live next to the corner shop, it occurred to me that they could be linked in a way which added to the realism of the show. So I continued like this (N.B. The letters OOV after the speech titles stand for 'out of vision', that is to say, the characters can be heard but not seen):

SCENE 2. STUDIO. CORNER SHOP. 10.05 AM
Len at the counter. He and Alf are listening to next door's row.

STAN (OOV)
(*Faint but audible*) Hey, that hurt!

HILDA (OOV)
It was meant to, you fat lump!

ALF
It's like livin' next to t'National Theatre at times.

The next example is a follow-up to a previous scene. In order to keep the various stories moving, the storyline writers, in their synopsis, split a long, slow scene between the two women into two parts and put a livelier scene in the Tilsleys' in between. This being the second half of the Emily–Flora duologue there is no need to re-set the scene with lengthy stage directions.

SCENE 12. STUDIO. EMILY'S LIVING-ROOM. 2.20 PM
Emily and Flora

He never stopped talking about you. Not from the day he met you. I've never known him like that over anyone before (*Emily's face is expressionless*). If he divorced her . . . and he could with being separated all this time . . . then you could . . . get married again and . . . (*She looks at Emily, tails off*)

EMILY

I don't think you understand. I was always . . . the most important thing in my life is honesty. I couldn't be dishonest with anyone I really love.

FLORA

He *must* have loved you! Why did he marry you if he didn't love you?

EMILY

I don't know (*A beat*). Flora, don't you see? That's not love as *I* understand it. It's not the kind of love I want. I don't expect . . . perfection. There were things I could have forgiven him but not that. Not saying that his wife was dead. That's wishing her dead and that's a terrible thing.

FLORA

(*Tearful*) What's going to happen to him?

EMILY

A friend said to me today that *we've* got our lives to live and she was right. I'm not heartless, really, but Arnold will survive. If he's lived all these years, knowing the truth and deceiving so many people . . . you, all his friends, me . . . then he can go on living. Perhaps, in some strange way, with a clearer conscience than either of us. He's forgiven himself. He's excused all the lies . . . deceits. You and I will always feel that somewhere we went wrong. Somehow, we're to blame. But I'm not going to let it be any worse than it need be. I'm not going to let him win. I'm going to make a cup of tea and then I'm going to collect all his clothes and . . . (*She's beginning to falter*) . . . I'm going to collect everything together and . . . call a taxi and you're going to take them away. Out of this house. Out of my life. (*She's breaking down*) I'm sorry!

Flora drops her head on her hands and weeps.

And from the crisis in the lives of two ordinary women to the no less harsh realities of life on the dole in the 1980s. The man still concussed by the shock of unemployment; his wife trying, by Lancashire understatement, to soften the blow.

SCENE 4. STUDIO. TILSLEYS' LIVING-ROOM 12.35 PM
Bert on the phone.

BERT

Yeah, I know. Weatherfield Chemicals are in t'same boat. I know, I saw 'em down t'Club. Any road, if you hear anything. You know what I can do. (*Ivy enters. He waves her to be quiet*) Have you got me home number . . .? Four three *two* nine! . . . Four three two nine, yeah! Right then! Keep smiling! . . . I will! (*Phone down*)

IVY

(*Could it be good news?*) Who was it?

BERT

Billy Lindley from Traffords.

IVY

Anything doing?

BERT

No, I'm just putting a few feelers out. Doesn't do any harm.

IVY

What about the Job Centre? (*He shakes his head, takes her shopping bag from her and starts to unpack it on to the table.*

158

She lets him) *I* think you're wasting your time till after Christmas. Nobody's going to bother till then.

BERT

You never know. You're probably right but you never know.

IVY

What are you doing *that* (*The unpacking*) for? Them's all got to go in the kitchen.

BERT

Oh aye! *He starts to pack again*

IVY

We haven't sorted out where we're going yet. Christmas and Boxing Day.

BERT

How d'you mean?

IVY

I mean Brian an' Gail. Are we going there or are they coming here. Not to mention Gail's mother. Which I wish I didn't have to.

BERT

Now look! No more flamin' hassles like that Sunday dinner!

IVY

I only want to sort it out!

BERT

Aye well! ((*Quietly*) We've got a lot to sort out.

IVY

I know, love! (*She picks up two or three unopened christmas cards*) When did *these* come?

BERT

I don't know. They were on t'mat when I come home. *Ivy is opening the envelopes. She reads the first.*

159

Would you credit it! Alice Taylor and Cyril! They never sent us one last year so I crossed 'em off the list, didn't I? There's always somebody!

Faced with the problem of the inconsequential scene – a few people gathered around the bar of the Rovers Return discussing nothing in particular – I always fall back on my own experience. Chatter of this kind always sounds more real if based on fact. The characters involved – Len and Eddie – enjoy talking about football so I chose football as a general topic. I saw the match between Arsenal and Manchester United so I wrote specifically about that. Here is how it went on to paper:

SCENE 8. STUDIO. ROVERS RETURN BAR. 1.25 PM
Annie and Bet behind the bar. Len and Eddie together. A few extras at the dartboard. Bet listening, Annie serving a customer.

LEN
You should 'a seen the gates just after the war. They got double what they get now. Sixty thousand was nothin'. I remember goin' to see Arsenal play United at Maine Road. There was ten thousand locked out – an' that was mid-week!

EDDIE
(*Smiling, to the apparently rapt Bet*) Spot the deliberate mistake, did you?

LEN
What deliberate mistake?

EDDIE
What deliberate mistake, he says! I may be an ignorant Scouse who's a few hundred years younger than you, squire, but even my limited intelligence tells me that United don't play at Maine Road.

160

LEN

That's where you're wrong, isn't it! They did then. They were bombed out at Old Trafford.

BET

(*Her hand on the pump. Mildly*) Did you have a bet on it?

EDDIE

No we flamin' didn't! (*To Len*) I stand corrected.

LEN

I reckon fifty thousand fellers played hookey from work that afternoon. It wasn't unemployment that was the problem in them days it was trying to get a factory working on a match day.

EDDIE

Why didn't they play 'em at night?

LEN

'Cos they didn't have floodlights then.

BET

(*To Eddie*) You're not doin' very well, love. If I was you I'd pack up while I was losin'.

EDDIE

I think I will. Give us a couple o' pints.

ANNIE

(*Drifting up*) Has the football talk finished?

BET

Looks like it, Mrs Walker.

ANNIE

Oh good! (*To Len and Eddie*) I *am* sorry but I find it excruciatingly boring.

LEN

So do I when I'm talking to ignoramuses like him! (*Eddie*)

Mind you, there's one or two players could get me excited. Not playin' football . . .

(*Mildly*) Now, Bet!

It isn't easy to judge the correct length of a script. It depends on many factors – the mood of the show (tragedy plays slow, comedy fast); the amount of silent action which, though described in only a few lines, may take minutes to run; the actors involved (Violet Carson in her prime could rattle through lines at machinegun speed); even the choice of directors – whilst some linger lovingly on an empty pint pot before starting the action in the Rovers Return, others jump from speech to speech without dwelling on the visual delights.

I conceded long ago that it is practically impossible to 'time' every script accurately. I rely on my instincts and, like all instincts, they are fallible. This particular script was too long and the first scene between Stan, Hilda and Eddie and the short 'overlap' section in the following Corner Shop scene had to be cut. I hope I will use them again. Some future storyline may give me an opportunity to re-vamp the 'cut' scenes. 'Waste not, want not' isn't an over-worked adage inside television but there is little more saddening for a writer than to see a scene he wrote with a great deal of relish lying abandoned on the floor of the director's office.

The most difficult line of any script is the last – the 'tag' line. *Coronation Street*, as I've noted, doesn't much practice the traditional cliffhangers. We believe in asking questions, in stimulating our viewers to talk about the show during the intervening days. I ended this particular script in the street itself. Hilda Ogden had just said goodbye to her visitor when something caught her eye:

Hilda watches as Emily, followed by Flora carries a pile of man's clothes and loads them into the taxi. A brief kiss between the women and the taxi goes. Emily goes back inside as Len turns the shop corner.

HILDA

Eh, did you see that?

LEN

What?

HILDA

Emily and that sister-in-law of hers. They've just taken all of Arnold's clothes away in a taxi.

LEN

Happen he's having 'em cleaned.

HILDA

All at once! Pull the other one! There's summat funny goin' on there!

Len smiles, shakes his head and walks on. Hilda goes in, reluctantly. The door closes. After a moment a corner of her curtain lifts and we see her face peering towards Emily's. Pull back and . . .

ROLL END CREDITS

The questions are posed. How will Hilda ferret out the truth? How will Emily take it when her tragedy becomes common knowledge? We leave the loose ends dangling unashamedly. We *want* our viewers to care, to come back next week and enjoy more episodes. Only that way will we lucky writers continue to enjoy writing them.

CHAPTER THIRTEEN

'Look in the glory hole! If it's not there I don't know where it is.'

Hilda Ogden

Thomas Fuller describes the memory as 'the treasure house of the mind wherein the monuments thereof are kept and preserved' but even so impressive an edifice has its glory hole. A top back room where each of us keeps those memorabilia no longer needed for day-to-day life. Items to be taken out and dusted only when some gust of nostalgia blows opens the door. And never to be found when a naïve journalist asks: 'There must have been one or two strange moments during *Coronation Street*'s life, Mr Kershaw. Can you think of any?'

As far as these relics, the stringless tennis rackets, faded school photographs and chipped china of *Coronation Street*'s past, are concerned, the anonymous child's definition of memory as 'the thing I forget with' may be nearer the mark. Not that they are wholly forgotten. If they were this chapter would never proceed beyond this point. Happily, all that is needed is a nudge, a word, a snatch of song and the glory hole door flies open and out they tumble. The first dusty, string-wrapped parcel is labelled 'Celebrations'.

As a producer I rarely enjoyed *Coronation Street*'s parties. Or, at least, their preparation. Each year, around the beginning of November, it was my job to set in motion the arrangements for the *Street*'s birthday party, normally held on the Friday evening nearest to 9 December. Catering, design and music were in other hands; my main task was to prepare the guest list. And a thankless job it was. Available space set an attendance ceiling of 120 Granada personnel, all of whom must have made a significant contribution to the programme in order to qualify for an invitation. Unfortunately there were differing ideas on what constituted a 'significant contribution'. The invitations would go out towards the end of November and during the two weeks up to the party night itself a walk through Granada's corridors was a gauntlet to be run. Strained smiles, hostile looks and even downright snubs greeted me from those who felt they'd qualified but hadn't been invited. It was, without doubt, the worst period of my year and the problem has only once been solved during the *Street*'s lifetime. For the show's thousandth performance, Granada's mammoth Studio 12 was thrown open, festooned and licensed and the company's entire staff gathered to celebrate.

When I wasn't producing, parties were another kettle of fish. These I could enjoy. Perhaps the most memorable – for obvious reasons – was the first. This was held in the Pineapple, behind Granada's studios, again on a Friday evening. Excitement ran high – hadn't we run for a whole year? – and the roistering was in full swing when the door opened and the Pineapple's only Friday night regular, a wizened ex-railwayman, found himself sucked into the revelry. Before he knew where he was he was pinioned at the bar between Pat Phoenix and Violet Carson and there he stayed, happily bemused, until the party ended when he staggered into the cold night air and stumbled back to one of the few 'two up and two downs' still remaining in the inner city. What happened then is anybody's guess but there's a probable scenario:

'Where d'you think *you've* been?' his nightgowned wife would demand.

'You're not going to believe this!' our happy wanderer would reply. And, when he went on to say that he had been drinking champagne with Ena Sharples and Elsie Tanner, the odds are she wouldn't.

Two months before our first birthday, *Coronation Street* was invited to switch on Blackpool Illuminations, at that time one of Britain's highest accolades. With clockwork precision

Blackpool's entertainment whiz-kids – amongst the best in the world – organized events for the night in early September when the ceremony was to take place. Itineraries, accommodation, table plans, speeches, all were arranged with meticulous attention to detail until, with a couple of weeks to go, I was informed that everything was under control. I relaxed, but not for long. A glance at the scripts to be produced the following week and transmitted on the Monday and Wednesday before the Lights ceremony had me picking up the telephone to ring John Finch, the writer. 'Come in!' I said, 'as fast as you can. We're in trouble.'

Half an hour later he was sitting in front of me, wondering what calamity had hit us now. 'Take a look at these,' I said, passing him the scripts. 'In Episode 78 we discover Ida Barlow has been knocked down by a double-decker bus. In Episode 79 we bury her. Two days later we switch on Blackpool Illuminations. We can't do it. The nation will still be in mourning!'

There was only one way out. John and I worked on two new episodes to be slotted into the schedules. Their main theme was 'Whatever has happened to Ida Barlow?' At the end of them she was missing but, to all intents and purposes, still alive, which allowed her death and funeral to be postponed and shown in the week after the Blackpool jollifications. The plan was put into operation. As they arrived the following Monday, an amazed cast were given the revised scripts to learn, Ida Barlow was kept alive for a further week and Noel Dyson, who played her, was able to join her fellow-artists on the rostrum as Violet Carson, Blackpool's favourite resident, threw the switch that lit the lights.

The whole day had been magic. Cast and production team travelled by train from Manchester to Preston where they transferred to an open double-decker bus for the triumphal ride into Blackpool itself. The welcome was stunning. Cheering crowds lined the entire route and a record throng waited in Talbot Square for our arrival. Police held back the fans as we struggled into a side door of the Town Hall. Lynne Carol, the *Street*'s Martha Longhurst was ahead of me as we erupted into the calm of the entrance hall. 'Marvellous!' she said, 'I've lived here all my life and they don't know who I am!' It was true. Lynne only had to take off her battered velour hat and her steel-rimmed spectacles and Martha Longhurst became a vivacious woman.

Once inside the Town Hall we were shown to the Mayor's Parlour for a welcome drink. The Mayor and his Mayoress greeted us. 'It's lovely to have you with us,' said Blackpool's no-nonsense first citizen. 'Get your feet up, have a nice cup o' tea while me and the missus go home and get usselves changed. As you know, there's a bit of a do on tonight so we've got to get us glad rags on.' The 'bit of a do' was not only the switching on of the Lights, Blackpool's biggest night of the year but a full-scale reception for the Commonwealth Parliamentary Conference which the resort was hosting at the time. That evening I stood at the entrance to the Great Chamber of the Town Hall and watched Mr Mayor, resplendent in evening dress, greet robed legislators from Nigeria, silk-suited senators from Canada and Australia, and parliamentarians from all over the Commonwealth in a manner which would have done credit to any of Her Majesty's Ambassadors. An impressive occasion, presided over by a most impressive gentleman in what, when it comes to putting on a show, is surely Britain's most impressive town.

From one impressive showbiz town to another. Hollywood – and the memory of how I never got there.

In the mid-1960s ABC (the American Broadcasting Corporation, not our own ABC Television) were starting production on what, to them, was a new venture – a twice-weekly, peak-time, drama serial on which was to be lavished as much time, money and production facilities as on the major drama series. The subject they had chosen was a loose adaptation and sequel to the Grace Metallious

Peyton Place novels. This, in American TV terms, was a startling innovation and its acceptance by one of the hyper-cautious 'majors' gives the lie to the widespread belief that in matters of popular entertainment the States invariably leads while the rest of the world tags behind. Listen to Doug Cramer, at that time one of American TV's most powerful men, talking about his earlier successes in an interview in *Campaign* of 14 November 1969. '*Peyton Place* was a serial,' he said, 'and the only comparable serial that had ever been seen at night was *Coronation Street*. Actually it was the success of *Coronation Street* that led us into doing *Peyton Place*. I'd been in England and after seeing it came back to ABC and said: "My God, look it's working and we really ought to do it." And that's when we got started on *Peyton Place*.'

It was this link which led to a suggestion from ABC that I should visit them in Hollywood. Had I gone I would, inevitably, have been drawn into discussions on production techniques, writing schedules and the other peculiarities of the *Street* and it was argued, quite reasonably, by Granada that if the States wanted a good twice-weekly serial they should buy ours and we shouldn't send people over there to help them make their own. This argument wasn't, however, without its holes. Whilst we all longed for the *Street* to be shown as widely as possible, most of us knew in our heart of hearts that it was too parochial, even by English standards, ever to make it big in the States. When, several years later, the show was given a short season in New York and Boston, this was confirmed. Although a cult formed amongst the more Anglicized sections of New York and Boston society, the show was Greek to most of its American viewers. Heaven knows what the Middle West would have made of us.

Doug Cramer's remarks did more than establish *Coronation Street* as the fore-runner of a new American TV genre; they confirmed a belief still held by those of us who work on the *Street* – the show is *not* a soap opera. Obviously Mr Cramer, who should know, did not consider *Peyton Place*

168

to be a soap opera and, for similar reasons, neither is the *Street*. The true soap opera is a production totally geared and subservient to the promotion of the product. Conversely, any programme which creates and follows its own standards and owes no allegiance to sponsorship of any kind cannot possibly be classed as 'soap'. Race meetings, cricket matches and show-jumping events which by association glorify products (usually hard drink or tobacco) are far more deserving of the label than *Emmerdale Farm* or *Coronation Street* will ever be. Although I was no longer treading the corridors of power when Angela Rippon produced *The Soap Opera Business* for the BBC in 1980 I should imagine that she was refused access to *Coronation Street* whilst making the documentary on the grounds that our show was not part of her subject matter. And quite right too.

There are other reasons why the lie should be given to the assertion that *Coronation Street* is a soap opera. One of the most important is that the show has rarely shirked issues which might affect the public sensibility. I don't refer to overt sex or bad language – far from being issues, these are usually no more than highly-spiced ingredients used to bring a dubious taste to an otherwise bland concoction. I am talking about matters of importance in everyday life on which there are widely differing opinions.

At an early story conference – in the spring of 1961 – such an issue dropped, almost unnoticed, on to the table. We had been planning our first Whit Monday episode in which the main story was a *Street* trip to Blackpool. I later wrote the episode which ended on the returning coach with Harry Hewitt, our bus inspector, proposing to and being accepted by Concepta Riley, the Rovers' Irish barmaid. It was whilst discussing this that Vince Powell dropped his bombshell.

'I suppose you all realize,' he said, 'that if we follow this story to its logical conclusion, we've got a mixed marriage on our hands?' He was absolutely right. Harry Hewitt had been played as strongly Protestant, Concepta Riley as devoutly Catholic.

We were faced with three choices. One, we laid bare all the complications and arguments of such a union; two, we married Harry and Concepta and ignored their differing beliefs or, three, we chickened out totally and backed away from the problem by breaking off the engagement. We decided to take the first choice and during the weeks up to the wedding we explored all the attendant difficulties of such a situation. As a result we were assailed by letters from Protestant and Catholic alike all complaining that we had shown a strong bias towards 'the other side'. It's difficult to win under such circumstances but at least we knew we hadn't taken the easy way out.

In January 1963 another subject was aired in the *Street*, again somewhat ahead of its time as far as popular drama was concerned. Len Fairclough, accused by a West Indian bus conductor of not paying his fare, reported the incident to his inspector friend Harry Hewitt when he appeared on the scene, with the result that the bus conductor was sacked. Len later admitted that he was in the wrong but the West Indian, when offered his job back, refused to return where he was obviously not trusted. Len and Harry were, quite rightly, the villains of this piece but it is interesting that the *Street* is still criticized for *never* including black or Asian characters. Blacks and Asians have, in fact, appeared many times although this would not be apparent from the scripts. It has long been a rule that all our coloured characters should be seen to be fully and happily integrated into the community. Which explains why one issue has, apparently, been shirked – namely, that successive producers have been loath to bring a coloured family into the *Street* itself. If this were to be done producers and writers would be forced by the very nature of the show to allow integration to develop at its own pace and to air a mixed bag of opinions on immigration and racialism. I am not alone in believing that such subjects are far too important simply to form one of many themes in a popular drama serial. What is more, in keeping faith with our existing characters, we would again be forced to put unhelpful comment into the mouths of fictional men and women who command a wide following among the serial's millions of viewers, with potentially dangerous effect. It is far easier to inflame the extremists with fictional support for their beliefs than to awaken the consciences of the uncaring with fictional moralities and it would be quite wrong, however strongly well-meaning bodies may urge us to do so, for an entertainment programme to run such risks and accept such responsibility.

Coronation Street does not usually tread such deep waters however and there are, happily, times when memory's doors open wider and allow a few lighter moments to escape. One of them concerned the *Street*'s treatment of reigning royalty.

From the outset *Coronation Street* was firmly planted in reality. Not for us the make-believe of the current American film where everything contemporary takes place in Centre City or the British play where, if the Prime Minister was mentioned, he was forever 'Lord Blessinghurst' or something similar. The *Street* allowed itself only one fiction and that was the name of its surrounding suburb. We chose 'Weatherfield' rather than Bury or Stockport or Irlams o' th' Height purely for purposes of protection. Had we placed the *Street* in a real borough we would have been bound by its by-laws and exposed ourselves to criticism every time we broke one. As it was we made our own. 'Weatherfield' became an autonomous state within the Greater Manchester conurbation. In all other respects, however, we were factual. We talked of 'going into Manchester', of genuine football teams, of real celebrities and when we spoke of the Prime Minister it was of Macmillan, Douglas-Home, Wilson, Heath, Callaghan or Mrs Thatcher. Moreover, although a tabu existed in our early days, if we wanted to talk about reigning royalty, we did. And we discussed them with that curious mixture of affection and intimacy with which they are regarded in most of Britain's working-class streets.

In the early summer of 1962 we were telling the story of a council proposal to re-name the street and Ena Sharples' valiant and successful battle to preserve the *status quo*. As part of her campaign she wrote for support to Prince Philip. The response was immediate. Sections of the Press accused us of lese-majesty. The day after the episode was screened the banner headlines in one of the daily tabloids screamed 'ENA AND THE DUKE' . . . 'QUESTIONS ASKED AT THE PALACE'. Exactly what questions no one quite knew because we never heard of any answers. We did, however, continue to discuss the royal family.

There are times, thankfully rare, when *Coronation Street* cannot tell its stories without outside help. I say 'thankfully rare' not from any lack of gratitude to the many who have assisted the programme – from dustmen to the Duke of Bedford – but from mistrust of the few who are either out to exploit the show or who let us down. The first group were well represented by a firm from whom we borrowed a large piece of machinery as a 'prop' in a factory where Dennis, wayward son of Elsie Tanner, was working at the time. I could have the machinery for nothing, I was told, plus all the help I needed, if the set could be photographed and used for publicity purposes. I explained that this was quite impossible and insisted that we pay a fair hiring fee. This was arranged and the episode went ahead. Several months later I was buttonholed by an engineer friend I hadn't met for some considerable time. 'I've been looking for you!' he said. 'I see you've gone into the advertising business!' and pulled out of his pocket a small leaflet which had apparently been circulated to all interested parties at at the time of our factory story. Underneath a photograph of the machine was the legend: 'Watch *Coronation Street* at 7.30 pm on Monday next and see our new product in action. All enquiries to . . .' Clever thinking but it shows how careful one has to be when running a popular programme!

The second group – those who don't quite come up to scratch – are perhaps deserving of more sympathy. The case that comes to mind also concerns Dennis Tanner – this time with a nine-foot python. During his brief career in show-business, Dennis befriended an exotic dancer who had been thrown out of her digs. Gallantly he offered her a night's lodging fondly believing that his mother was away until the following morning. And fondly believing, too, that the dancer was alone. Taking advantage of Dennis's generosity, the dancer smuggled her python partner into the Tanners' where he was left in a cardboard box on the kitchen table. It was obvious, when the story was planned, that no one on Granada's studio staff was qualified to handle reptiles of this size, and help was sought from the local zoological gardens. On the day a rather supercilious snake handler arrived complete with nine-foot charge.

What did we wish his python to do? he asked. We explained that the snake would lie in the bottom of his box until, in the middle of the night, Elsie would return, switch on the light and look inside a duplicate box on her kitchen table. She would then scream at which point we would cut to a camera poised over the genuine box on a 'props' table at the side of the studio. The shot we wanted was of the disturbed python rearing its ugly head. Or beautiful head, according to whether or not one happens to be an ophiolater. We asked the snake-handler if this was within his powers.

'Is that all you want it to do?' he asked, implying that if we wanted the snake to ride a unicycle whilst juggling with a set of Indian clubs that, too, could be arranged. No, we insisted, that was all we wanted. Simply goad the snake into action at the appropriate moment. The floor manager gave his final instructions. Just before the Elsie scream he would cue the snake handler who would then, we were assured, rouse the snake into activity by tickling him with a stick he had brought for the very purpose. The scene started, the moment came, the cue was given and the snake handler began to tickle. Unfortunately the python, which should have been enlivened by the hot studio lights, had decided to take his afternoon nap. The tickle turned into a prod, the prod into a jab and the jab into a full-scale attack before the red-faced snake-handler was dragged bodily away from the 'props' table and a shot taken of an apparently dead reptile curled at the bottom of a cardboard box. A few minutes later the embarrassed zooman slunk with his charge out of the studio, covered in shame, and we resigned ourselves to a shoal of letters asking why Elsie had been so frightened of a lifeless python.

By no means all our problems stemmed from outside the programme. Many of them were mechanical. A camera going 'on the blink' in the middle of a taping session could create havoc in the studio whilst a fault in the tape – only to be discovered on a spot check after the episode had been completed – has been known to cost us an episode. Normally the cast and studio staff are kept until the spot check has been made but I well remember one occasion when Arthur Lowe, the *Street*'s Leonard Swindley, believing the 'all clear' to have sounded, left the studio and had to be dragged from the London train at Manchester's Piccadilly Station, driven back to Granada and made to re-record several scenes before finally been allowed to go home! Our main worries, however, are human and the worst worry of all is illness.

Whilst it is probably true that the saying 'the show must go on' was coined by a theatre manager rather than an actual performer it is even truer that no one tries harder to do his or her job than the average artist. I have known frail actresses turn up for work in physical conditions which would have kept dockers on the sick list for weeks. Nevertheless there are occasions when even the strongest willed must fall and that dreaded telephone call from an artist's doctor to the effect that X will not be in that week, strikes terror into the heart of the toughest producer. One corner of my memory's glory hole holds what I have always thought of as my luckiest escape.

We were in January 1965 and everything was going swimmingly when, one Tuesday morning, out of a cold blue sky, came the chilling news that Miss X would not be fit to work for the rest of that week. This would have been bad news at any time but on this particular week Miss X was the central character in the main story and her loss tore huge holes in both episodes. There was only one thing to do – rewrite. Whilst my secretary contacted both the writers involved and told them to hotfoot it to the studios I had a quick flip through the scripts to see if any ideas sprang to mind. None did, so I settled down to wait for the arrival of the writers in the hope that three heads would be better than one. Whilst I waited, with my mind on my problem, I read the morning's mail. Suddenly, in front of me, in crabbed handwriting on cheap notepaper, lay the solution. A letter from an elderly lady in North London (with no address but with an apologetic postscript giving a telephone number 'just in case') pointed the way to salvation. Why not, wrote the lady, let Len Fairclough, then a lonely widower, advertise for a housekeeper? What usually happaned, the lady added, was that at least one of the applicants would have either left her husband or have been thrown out by him and would rely on such a job to provide a roof over her head. Holding my breath I checked the scripts. Yes, Peter Adamson, who played Len Fairclough, was in that week's cast. What was more, his 'living-room' was one of the five sets to be used. Had the old lady been in the room I would have hugged her. By the time the writers arrived I had worked out the bare bones of the story, our casting director had been alerted to find the necessary extra artists to play successful and unsuccessful applicants and by mid-afternoon the amended scripts were in the typing pool awaiting duplication. Before they went home that night each artist was given the rewritten material to learn for the following morning. On that day the new artists joined us and two days later, on the Friday, two episodes were made containing a story which had not been thought of before that fateful Tuesday, only seventy-two hours previously.

Ah, I can hear you saying, but what happened to the old lady? Fear not! My first duty, after reading her letter and before checking anything, had been to get in touch with her. The most surprised lady in Britain listened to me as, over the telephone, I told her I would like to buy her story and offered the current going rate for professional storylines which she happily accepted.

Let me stress, 'the going rate for *professional* storylines'. There was no scale at that time, nor is there now, for amateur storylines. In fact producers, particularly those of long-running serials, positively discourage the general public from submitting story ideas and for a very sound reason. There is nothing more embarrassing than to receive, usually from a loyal viewer, a suggestion for a story that has already been planned by us and is going through the pipeline. And this is by no means a rare coincidence. Many of our viewers are as bound up in our stories as are the production team itself and it is only logical that our imaginations should wander along the same paths particularly when the shared idea is an extension of a story currently on the screen.

I always felt that when I wrote back explaining that the correspondent's idea was already being used there were faint mutterings (and sometimes not so faint) of 'Oh yes? I've heard that one before!' What the helpful viewer (and many of them *are* trying to be helpful) fails to realize is that what he sees on the screen has been planned up to three months earlier and there are, at any one time, a couple of dozen episodes in existence in various stages of production. These twenty-odd episodes may well contain his idea, thought up by the production team months previously whereas *his* version was sparked off by the episode he saw the night before he wrote in. Even if a proffered suggestion has not been considered by the *Street* story conference it will be seen that by the time the viewer has his bright idea it is often too

176

late to slot it into our forward planning. The message therefore is – don't send story ideas to programmes such as *Coronation Street*. It can only lead to embarrassment and ill-feeling. And the lady from North London? This was explained to her and to her eternal credit she has never sent in another suggestion. She realized, as did we, that her one success was a phenomenon. This was the classic case of the right idea landing on the right desk at exactly the right time and the odds against this happening again are astronomical.

Apparent reality has always been the stock-in-trade of *Coronation Street*. It has already been explained that the show is a digest of the events of a hundred streets without (we hope) the boring bits and it would be quite wrong for us to claim total reality. One aspect of real life which is however part and parcel of *Coronation Street* is its slight untidiness. Whilst in the Hollywood epic hero and heroine glide effortlessly through shot and shell, mouth each syllable with impeccable diction and show perfect faces to their adoring fans, in real life people bump against chairs, stumble over words and, on occasion, smudge their lipstick. And so they do in *Coronation Street*, mainly, and fortunately, because it's difficult to achieve perfection under a five-day schedule. I recall at one of Granada's informal producers' lunches sitting between SLB, as Lord Bernstein is more familiarly known and Jeremy Isaacs, now Head of Channel 4, then a fellow producer. Jeremy, always ready for a little harmless 'stirring', congratulated me on the high standard of 'fluffs' in *Coronation Street*. (For the uninitiated, a 'fluff' is where an artist stumbles over or momentarily forgets a line.)

'Ah!' I said, fighting back. 'Ah! We're rather proud of those! Mistakes like that bring us nearer to the audience, make us more human!'

SLB leaned over and joined in the joke. 'Good thinking!' he said. 'Have you ever thought of writing a few fluffs into the script?'

I hadn't and fortunately I've never had the need although I'm constantly amazed by the degree of polish brought to many of the *Street*'s episodes on such a meagre ration of rehearsal time. Things, of course, are better now than they were. In the early days electronic marvels were still around the corner. We recorded the episodes on videotape but we had available to us only the most primitive methods of editing together pieces of tape. For this reason programmes were recorded in one take and if a sound boom or a camera strayed into shot fifteen million viewers saw it happen.

Nowadays our methods are more sophisticated and these unexpected pleasures are denied to the modern audience. Although, in the old days, calamities were overcome with the tapes still rolling – if an actor forgot a line, somebody else would *ad lib* until it was remembered – everyone knew that some day a disaster would occur of such magnitude that it could not possibly be left on the tape to be shown to the public. When that happened the director involved would be called upon to order 'Stop tape!' and thereby involve the company's engineers in their first exercise of what was called 'knife and fork' editing. The offending piece of action would be cut from the tape and the two separate lengths literally stuck together. Later the practice became prevalent. When viewers noticed a slight hiccup in the programme, that would be the result of a 'knife and fork' edit.

It so happened that I was present in the *Street*'s Studio 2 control room the day those dread words 'Stop tape!' were first spoken in Granada. All was going well under the direction of Howard Baker, now one of Granada's senior producers, when we began to notice the intrusion of background music under the sound track. This was, apparently, much more noticeable on the studio floor and came, we later discovered, from Count Basie's band in full flow in the neighbouring Studio 6. Even walls as well soundproofed as Granada's were no match for the Count and his brass section. We ignored the melodic invasion for a little while but it was obviously unsettling the cast and the crunch came when Violet Carson, at the bar of the Rovers, suddenly broke off in full flow, lifted her eyes appealingly to the control room window and through the open microphone said, 'I just can't take any more!'

All eyes turned to Howard Baker, the man in the hot seat. What would he do? Would he tell his floor manager to urge Violet on with the next line and hope the audience would see her plea as a prayer from Ena to her Maker to relieve her from the horrors of the Demon Drink? A glance at the monitors made up Howard's mind. It was obvious that not only Violet but everyone in the studio had totally lost concentration. He swallowed hard and took the irrevocable step. 'Stop tape!' he said, the tape stopped rolling and another little piece of history was made.

Another piece of nostalgia lies on the glory hole floor. A tattered photograph of the classic row, fought out on the street, between Ena Sharples and Elsie Tanner. Episode 93B, if my memory serves me right – the 'B' signifying that this was the second episode after the start of the actors' strike of 1961. What few of our viewers will remember is that, in those days, the street was built in the studio and the cobblestones painted on the studio floor. It was only when electronic editing was fully adopted and it became a comparatively simple process to produce our shows in pieces to be joined together by the miracle men in the editing suite, that we turned our minds to the possibility of building our *Street*, Hollywood-style, in God's open air. There were, however, what we thought insuperable difficulties in finding a suitable site. Not realizing that this day would ever come we had made a substantial rod for our own backs. *Coronation Street*, we had established, was a short thoroughfare of seven houses flanked by a pub and a corner shop, lying between Rosamund Street, a busy main road and, at the shop end, Viaduct Street. The problem was that Viaduct Street's far boundary was a fictional but massive railway

179

viaduct which lay at right angles to the bottom of our street. Obviously building our own viaduct on an outside lot was out of the question but where were we to find a location with such a ready-made feature? Fate positively beamed on us.

One day I was telephoned by Granada's General Manager. 'Come and have a walk round the back of the complex,' he said. 'I've something interesting to show you.' He led me into Grape Street which runs alongside the studios to a pair of high solid gates set into a high brick wall. Opening a small wicket gate in one of the larger gates he beckoned me to enter and I stepped through into yesterday. There in front of me was a large cobblestoned area bounded on two sides by a high brick wall, on a third by a bonded warehouse and on the fourth by – and I could scarcely believe my eyes – a railway viaduct. As if that wasn't enough: 'We can rent this area,' he said, 'and we can build on it.' Not only had we found the impossible, it had turned up in our own backyard.

Work started immediately. The studio was weather-proofed and erected at the right angle to the existing viaduct. Unfortunately, as eagle-eyed viewers will have noticed, this meant that the cobblestones, instead of running parallel with the fronts of our houses, ran at an angle. This was a minor setback and gladly accepted. A greater misfortune lay in the fact that our studio set of the *Street* had been scaled down in size. However, odd though this looked to the naked eye, when seen through the TV camera, the houses appeared to be of normal proportions.

The studio set, weather-proofed or not, didn't last long. A severe winter played havoc with the lath and board houses and the following year I asked for, and was given, enough money to build the façade of the *Street* in brick. This would have been an opportunity to scale up the size of the houses but unhappily there was only enough working space to allow a street of the same dimensions to be built. What we did do, however, was to build the back walls, backyards and back alley behind the original façade. All the houses now have a front and a back but no innards.

As a writer I enjoy using the 'outside lot'. Its use in conjunction with sets such as the Rovers Return and the corner shop gives a realistic movement to the show which is difficult to obtain in the studio alone. On Emily Bishop's wedding day I had Bet Lynch waving her off to the Register Office, turning to see a taxi pull up outside the Rovers and walking inside the pub shouting 'Mrs Walker! Your taxi's here!' The first part had been shot outside on the Monday morning, the second part in the studio on the following Friday afternoon but in the completed sequence, like Ernie Wise's hairline, you couldn't see the join.

Those few words 'as a writer' spark off all kinds of memories, most of them warm, few of them unhappy. It is a sad comment on the history of work and the human species that so few of us thoroughly enjoy our chosen occupation. And that of those few only a tiny proportion can put their hands on their hearts and say that their work gives them more satisfaction than could any other. I count myself fortunate to be amongst that tiny minority.

Obviously the ideal occupation must satisfy both the material and the spiritual needs of the individual. There is little future in doing the job one loves if one starves to death in the process. Nor is there much point in making masses of money from a hated labour which devours the whole of one's days, one's energy and one's finer feelings.

Writing is one of those rare professions which meets these ideal conditions. What is more, unlike so many other jobs, it can be practised at any time of the day or night, Sundays or Bank Holidays without breaking the law or the principles of trades unionism. Which leads me to another thought. I don't know what I have done to deserve it but I am, at this moment, a self-employed trade unionist. It isn't easy to be a card-carrying brother and a member of the National Federation of the Self-Employed at one and the same time but up to a few years ago I was just such a schizophrenic. Not that other trade unions take us all that seriously. From what I hear each time a Writers' Guild representative gets up to speak at the Trades Union Congress he is greeted with howls of derision. Apparently there is a widespread belief amongst the movement that all writers are filthy rich. Actually only a few are – the majority are poverty-stricken – and our average earnings would prompt any other union, with the possible exception of Equity, to declare an eternal strike.

That writers can form a union at all is little short of amazing. Most of us are heavily individualistic. Not only that, we are constantly in competition with each other. The Guild was formed, as I saw it, to fight the worst excesses of exploitation and, so far, it has been highly successful. One of its great achievements was to win for its members, fragmented though they are, a profitable pension scheme supported by BBC and ITV companies alike. Such matters are, I feel, the function of such a Guild as ours and it performs them admirably. There are, of course, those members who would turn us into yet another militant group spending less time writing than fighting the war of 'us' and 'them' but fortunately they are still in the (vociferous) minority.

The writer's life is not invariably elysian. There are frustrating times like the eleven-week strike of 1979 when, for the entire duration of the dispute, I didn't earn a single penny. My Guild was not involved in any way but we suffered all the same and for all I know the union who called the strike never gave us a moment's thought. I searched for signs of brotherhood but none was to be seen.

Thankfully such tribulations are rare. It was as a producer that I really felt the weight of strained labour relations.

As 'Johnny-in-the-middle' it was my job to get the programme back on to the rails as soon as the dispute was over and this was by no means as easy as it might sound. I remember, the first day back from a two-week dispute, meeting a quite senior engineer in one of Granada's corridors. I scowled at him – the strike had been an infernal nuisance and I felt I had the right to scowl – but he smiled back. 'Don't look like that, Harry!' he said. 'It's all over, you've had a nice rest and all you've got to do is start again where you left off.' He was a nice chap and I liked him but I was appalled by his ignorance. Didn't he realize that, if we *did* start where we left off, everything would be two weeks out of gear? We were planned three months ahead and artists who had been booked to join us during that period would be wanted two weeks later when, like as not, they would be working for the BBC and not available to us. The episode carefully planned for Christmas Day would then appear, to the public surprise, in the second week in January. Anniversaries, birthdays, covered in our planning would all be two weeks late. Cast holidays – many of them booked in advance – would need to be cancelled and re-arranged. Yet here was a highly paid fellow-employee who thought that all I had to do was pick up where I'd left off. He was lucky I only scowled at him!

What in fact had to happen was a total rewriting of not only the episodes we had failed to record during the dispute but also the next few pairs in a way that brought us back to our time-scale as soon as possible. This meant that, say, eight scripts would be torn up and their story content squeezed into a single pair of episodes. Moreover, several following scripts would need substantial re-writing to take care of the amended 'loose ends' which are ever-present in any serial.

This particular incident – the meeting with the engineer – illustrated the two quite separate worlds which exist within television. Not merely different but widely differing. On the one hand men and women who create a fictional world; on the other individuals who deal only in hard fact. One group spinning words, the other creating and exploiting electronic wizardry. It is difficult to imagine two more dissimilar sections of the human species and yet here they were side by side, all doing their varied utmost to make the best programmes they could. And, sadly, knowing little about each other's problems, feelings or aspirations.

It would be wrong to say that either side was blameless in this respect although it is true that there was more movement and therefore more transfer of knowledge from the engineering and service departments to the production side of the business than vice versa. Many designers and cameramen become directors and producers but I don't know a single writer, producer or director who has become a senior engineer. This lack of mutual understanding is saddening when one considers how dependent both sides are, one on the other. Without the production side the engineers would sit twiddling their thumbs. Without the engineers my scripts would remain words on paper and would never be translated into a visual performance.

The word 'misunderstanding' releases another memory. One March in the programme's middle years, I was coerced by Sir Denis Forman, then Granada's Programme Controller, into representing ITV at a seminar held for the day-release students of the Yorkshire and Derbyshire coalfields. I say 'coerced' as Sir Denis (by far the most persuasive executive I have ever met) forgot to mention that the date he had given me was not merely a simple day in April but also Easter Monday. By the time I found out it was too late and, deciding to make the best of it, I took my wife and daughter along for the weekend. The venue was Skegness, the wind was cold and blustery but, heigh-ho, I was there and on the Sunday afternoon I decided to look at the lie of the land. I was shown around the Miners' Holiday Camp by the secretary, a grizzled, stiff-backed ex-miner, who nonchalantly told me that he had another £600,000 in the kitty but he couldn't decide what to spend it on. And, looking at the size of the place, with its facilities and its luxury bars every hundred yards or so, I could well appreciate his predicament. As I left him to return to the hotel he invited me to a get-together buffet to be held in the camp that evening for the students – mainly young miners – and their wives. I accepted his invitation, remembering from past occasions, that there was always something to be gained by assessing one's audience (or in this case, as it turned out, opponents) in advance.

The weekend – the highspot of the miners' academic year – was on this occasion devoted to popular entertainment, and speakers and panels had been invited from the worlds of cinema, theatre, radio and television. The BBC's television representative was John Hopkins, later to be greatly acclaimed for his quartet of plays, *Talking to a Stranger*, but at that time, one of *Z-Cars*' most distinguished writers. I knew John well. He had been a floor-manager at Granada in my early days there, and we had discussed the writer's life over many a cup of coffee in the staff canteen. Our careers had forced us apart and it was pleasant to renew our acquaintance over the telephone a few days before we were due at Skegness. Finding that we had similar views we decided to share a platform rather than do the 'us and them' act more often performed by BBC and ITV. John wasn't arriving from London until late on Sunday evening so I went to the shindig on my own.

I appeared to be the only representative of the entertainers in a sea of miners but, while the initial encounters were somewhat wary, the atmosphere soon eased and, at the end of the evening, I found myself sharing a table and several gallons of beer with three miners and their wives. All three men were in their late twenties, all avid to learn and all obviously taking the weekend very seriously indeed. It being a social occasion their wives were allowed to ask flippant questions about the *Street* and its characters but the following day the gloves came off with a vengeance and any lady who enquired about Ena's hairnet was angrily howled down. Answering one antagonistic question, I recall, I was foolish enough to add that I enjoyed a good night's sleep and was told in no uncertain terms that, as I was responsible for a programme seen by over twenty million people twice a week, I had no right to sleep well. That, however, was on the Monday. On this Sunday evening, the exchanges were less biting. Until, that is, I caught one of the young miners eyeing me from head to toe from his neighbouring seat. I looked down, wondering if my clothing was properly adjusted. It was so I waited for the next question.

It was a surprising one. 'Might I ask if you're wearing that suit when you speak to us tomorrow, Mr Kershaw?' he asked. The suit in question was charcoal grey, formal and the only outfit I had brought with me so I said I was.

'Good for you!' he said and, turning to his two companions, 'Good for him, eh?'

'Aye, good for him!' they both agreed. I waited politely for an explanation and sure enough, it came.

'We had that Arnold Wesker talking to us on Saturday,' he said, 'telling us about his People's Theatre and his culture and that! In a pullover and an open-necked shirt and a pair of corduroy slacks!' He looked for confirmation to his two companions and they scowled their disapproval. 'He knows what he can do with his culture!' Which explains why the word 'misunderstanding' unleashed this particular memory. It is a sad reflection on human understanding that Arnold Wesker, who had so much to offer, should have his views so cavalierly dismissed for the sake of a charcoal grey suit. Whether or not my three miners spoke for all their colleagues, I don't know. I suspect they did and if I'm right then perhaps Mr Wesker is also at fault for failing to understand the conventional aspirations of the people he sought to reach. I have no other comment to make – I simply tell the story as it happened.

When I got back to the hotel that night I rang John Hopkins. 'What are you wearing tomorrow?' I asked. As he pondered, a little devil sat on my shoulder. 'He's from the BBC,' the devil whispered, 'tell him to wear a pullover and a pair of corduroy slacks!' But he was a friend of mine and I told him to wear a suit.

The following day, John Hopkins and I were savaged by

a hundred bloodthirsty miners. And we were both wearing dark suits. God knows what they did to Arnold Wesker.

The glory hole is almost empty. A few dusty parcels remain, stuck in an inaccessible corner and one or two bits and pieces lie waiting to be picked up and smiled over. The sight of Sir John Betjeman, our Poet Laureate, guest at a special *Street* lunch, as wide-eyed and bewitched as a schoolboy entertained by the England soccer team. At another Granada lunch, sitting next to the late Sir Alfred Hitchcock and listening as he explained to me, step by step, how he built up the suspense in *Psycho*. A Press conference in an Amsterdam hotel to preview *Coronation Street*'s showing in Holland and the carafe of water to which I helped myself liberally and later discovered to be a carafe of Genevre, the local spirit. Little wonder that the Dutch journalists asked their questions in a more precise English than I could offer in reply. And, finally, tied in faded ribbon, the letters offering Ena a home when Leonard Swindley kicked her out of the Glad Tidings Mission.

So much for the past. The question remains – what of the future? If, indeed, there is to be one.

CHAPTER FOURTEEN

'The end of *Coronation Street* is nigh!'

Daily Express, Daily Mail, Daily Mirror, Sun, Daily Telegraph, News of the World, Guardian, New Statesman, Punch, old Uncle Tom Cobley and all

On Monday, 12 December 1960, three days after the launching of *Coronation Street*, another Granada programme, also destined to be a long runner, appeared for the first time. This was *All Our Yesterdays*, a look at events of the same week twenty-five years previously, through the newsreels of the time, presided over by the admirable Brian Inglis. I found it entertaining, nostalgic and, in one respect, strangely helpful.

Whenever I was asked, during my years as producer, how long I thought *Coronation Street* would last, *All Our Yesterdays* helped me with my answer. If, I would say, it is true that a programme can usefully survive as long as its supply of usable material lasts then *Coronation Street*, drawing as it did on the whole of the human condition, could carry on until the end of the world. *All Our Yesterdays*, I would add, could keep going for a further twenty-five years. Unhappily Granada ruined the joke by taking *All Our Yesterdays* off the air in March 1973 and now, if I am asked that same question, I can only fall back on my original premise – *Coronation Street*'s raw material being nothing more specialized than people, the programme could be around for a long time. But, if that is true, why take off *All Our Yesterdays*? What better source of material than the continuing past? The truth was that this source didn't dry up, it simply changed character. When the programme started in 1960 it concerned itself with 1935 onwards and those dramatic years running up to the Second World War. Four years later that war, with its vast reserves of film material, had started but the excitement of post-war recovery evaporated and in 1973 Granada faced the prospect of dealing with two boring years, 1948 and 1949, when the most gripping items on the newsreels of the day were the battles between Aneurin Bevan and Charles Hill over the make-up of the National Health Service or, at the other end of the spectrum, the parade of pulchritude at the current beauty contest. Neither of which were the stuff of *All Our Yesterdays*. And so it was that the programme, reluctantly, was taken off the air.

No such criterion governs *Coronation Street*. The show does not feed on war, high excitement and the heady stuff of history. It nourishes itself on the trivia of human life, on birth, marriage and death, on making ends meet and looking after the kids. Trivia which are no less with us during the years of peaceful boredom than during the years of war.

If raw material is no problem, what else might bring about the end of *Coronation Street*? Some programmes rely heavily on a single ingredient – a personality, a particular actor, a writer, even a producer and if this indispensable being moves on to other things, the programme disappears with him. Again, *Coronation Street* does not fall within this category. Many people have moved on and the *Street* has not only survived but continued to thrive. Which is not to say that some losses are not sorely felt. To lose artists of the calibre of Arthur Leslie and Graham Haberfield would be a body blow to any drama programme but *Coronation Street* has so much in-depth acting strength that it can absorb such deprivations. The loss of Jack Rosenthal, Peter Eckersley, John and Brian Finch from the writing team might have seemed insuperable but the infusion of Leslie Duxbury, Julian Roach, John Stevenson, Barry Hill, Peter Whalley and Tony Perrin guaranteed the succession. It might be argued, too, that the number of people with both the appetite and the ability to produce the show is severely limited yet Bill Podmore, the current man at the top and the show's *seventeenth* producer, has all the qualifications for the job in full measure. Under Bill's guidance the *Street*, far from declining into a creaky old age, has gone from strength to strength.

It would be unwise to state, categorically, that *Coronation Street* will last for ever. Accidents happen even in the best regulated society and some whim of management might well bring the programme to an untimely end. Nor is it enough to proclaim its immortality because it is an institution. Not all institutions are sacred to all men, and a generation which can put *The Times* to sleep for over a year and send cricketers on to a floodlit field in yellow pads is surely capable of anything. To go even further, institutions tend by their nature to be old and television is in the forefront of that movement which would clear out the old to allow the young to flourish. Here, however, *Coronation Street* enjoys two decided advantages.

A television serial gains in strength as the years go by. Unlike the series, with its separate, self-contained stories on a common theme or about a single character, the serial, by its inexorability, gains in respect and credibility as it keeps pace with the life of the viewer. Many series are suspended in time. Their heroes and heroines are ageless but if fiction can hold back the years, fact puts lines on the faces of those heroes and sooner or later Father Time nudges the programme's producers into submission. Not so the serial. Len Fairclough is as convincing in 1980 as he was in 1960 not in spite of but *because* of having aged twenty years.

There are hybrid versions which seek the best of both worlds. These are the series/serials which unfold, in weekly fifty-minute episodes, some continuing family saga. A sense of reality is hard to come by for such programmes because of their broken nature. It is more difficult to become involved with characters who disappear for months on end than with those who appear on the screen, God or unions permitting, twice a week through spring, summer, autumn and winter.

Coronation Street, unlike these hybrids, is a pure serial. Moreover it is – and here I draw on outside opinion – the best of its genre. Not because of its acting and writing strengths although these play a large part, but because it has never failed (except briefly through no fault of its own) to produce 104 half-hour episodes per year, rain or shine. And – perhaps more important – it has resisted every attempt to increase its weekly output. Two twenty-five-minute episodes are as much as body, soul and any acceptable standards can endure and by restricting output to this level, successive producers have been able to produce what they like to think is a quality article. I am convinced that there will always be a place on British television for a long-running serial and as long as *Coronation Street* can continue to be the best of its genre, there is no reason why it should not hold that place.

The key to how long *Coronation Street* will endure lies in that last sentence: as long as it continues to be the best of its genre. How then can it fall from grace? The answer is alarmingly simple. There is still, after more than two decades, a vitality, an excitement, a pride in *Coronation Street* which override all the programme's handicaps. Let that vitality and excitement wither, that pride languish and the end could be in sight. If the time comes when the story conference accepts any story without debate in a rush to get to the pub, when writers dash off the scripts merely for the money, when those scripts are translated on to the screen by directors and actors who wish they were doing something else, the end will be in sight. But there is no sign of this happening in the foreseeable future. Today I finish this book. Tomorrow I go to Manchester for what will be *Coronation Street*'s 350th story conference. Assuredly, it will be as argumentative, as caustic, as possessive and as joyful as it has ever been.

If *Coronation Street* possesses one quality which both explains its past and secures its future it is its unpretentiousness. The show has always been able to laugh at itself, has always realized that life is not black and white, but full of sunshine and shadows. The characters too have never been merely saints or sinners but little bits of both at times and mainly in between. And those of us who have been lucky enough to work on it have never, in spite of the programme's phenomenal success, claimed it to be more than it is.

As my mother said so many years ago in that darkened cinema: 'It's only a story.'

But *what* a story!